A Life in School

DATE

OTHER BOOKS
BY JANE TOMPKINS

❧

West of Everything: The Inner Life of Westerns
Sensational Designs: The Cultural Work of American Fiction
Reader-Response Criticism: From Formalism to Post-Structuralism (editor)

A Life in School

WHAT THE TEACHER LEARNED

Jane Tompkins

Addison-Wesley
Reading, Massachusetts

Library of Congress Cataloging-in-Publication Data

Tompkins, Jane P.
   A life in school : what the teacher learned / Jane Tompkins.
     p. cm.
   Includes bibliographical references (p.).
   ISBN 0-201-91212-0
   ISBN 0-201-32799-6 (pbk)
   1. Tompkins, Jane P. 2. Teachers—United States—Biography.
  3. Teaching—United States. 4. Education—United States—Experimental methods. I. Title.
   LA2317.T65A3 1996
   371.1'0092—dc20
   [B]   96-31326
                                            CIP

Cover design by Suzanne Heiser
Text design by Merrick Hamilton
Set in 10-point Bitstream Transitional 521 by Merrick Hamilton

1 2 3 4 5 6 7 8 9- DOH-0100999897
First printing, September 1996
First paperback printing, August 1997

Find us on the World Wide Web at
http://www.aw.com/gb/

To my mother, my first teacher

CONTENTS

A *Life in School*

PREFACE

At the age of forty-nine, having spent most of my conscious years inside the walls of academic institutions, I realized I no longer had much use for the things I'd learned in school. By this I don't mean that what I had learned was worthless, but that the subjects I had studied and taught, and the way I had studied and taught them, were secondary to the real concerns of my life.

This realization followed upon a period of internal change, still going on, in which I gradually became aware that life was not as I had always taken it to be but something very different. How different was only just beginning to dawn. It became clear to me that I was not in my life to make a career for myself but to give something, though what, specifically, I didn't yet know. I could tell that school was no longer the place for me. And even while I continued to draw a salary and teach classes in the university, I had, in some sense, graduated and was living in another world.

This book looks back on my life in school with an eye to understanding at least some of it: recording what it was like, for me, to be a teacher and a student. Though much of what I have to say is painful, my intent is not to repudiate that life but to examine it in a way that may be useful, especially to those who work within the present educational system. Because I am a product of that system, it would be ungrateful and even dishonest for me to turn my back on it. It made me what I am. Still, much of what I have to say is critical, for I am still smarting from wounds sustained long ago. My chief concern is that our educational system does not focus on the inner lives of students or help them to acquire the self-understanding that is the basis for a satisfying life. Nor, by and large, does it provide the safe and nurturing environment that people need in order to grow. My teachers have not been of the usual kind—a dog, a course of massages, Alzheimer's patients, homeless people, Buddhist meditation, a nondenominational, charismatic African-American church. The experiences that have meant the most to me have taken forms that are antithetical to what we mean when we refer to learning in an academic sense. Overcoming my resistance to these nonintellectual modes of knowing has been the work of my life in recent years. What was lacking in me—respect for the whole human organism, emotions, body, and spirit, as well as mind—is what is lacking in American education as well.

It may seem strange that there are so few references here to books on education theory, so little attempt to set my experience against the background of classroom practice as it's described in the literature. For a long time I was at a loss to explain this myself. All I knew was, I had no desire to pick up a book on teaching—in fact, I had a positive aversion to doing so—and I couldn't even muster the energy to feel guilty about it. Now I realize that this refusal to read about my subject *was* my subject. It came from a need to finally trust myself. It was to my own experience that I needed to turn for enlightenment. For it was the failure of my education to turn my attention to that experience, so that I might know myself and thus be able to rely on myself; it was this failure, which was ultimately my own, that I needed to come to terms with and, in writing this book, to compensate for.

Preface

In some areas of life, perhaps, it is possible to learn what one needs to know from reading about what other people have done. Perhaps teaching is one of them. But for me, very few books I have read on the subject approached it in a way that spoke to my condition. Indeed, there are only four: Paolo Freire's *Pedagogy of the Oppressed*, Parker Palmer's *To Know as We Are Known*, Sylvia Ashton-Warner's *Teacher*, and Maria Montessori's *The Absorbent Mind*. All share a vision of life that transcends the concerns of any particular educational system and shapes the author's conception of what an education is. Freire's book strikes a blow for political justice; Palmer's holds up an image of true community; Ashton-Warner's is dedicated to free self-expression; and Montessori's to the growth of whole human beings. What they have in common is a commitment to the sacredness of life, and a fearlessness to speak on its behalf. What I take from them is courage to speak the truth about my experience and the hope that what I record here will render the experience of others more alive.

What I would like to see emerge in this country is a more holistic way of conceiving education—by which I mean a way of teaching and learning that is not just task-oriented but always looking over its shoulder at everything that is going on around. Such a method would never fail to take into account that students and teachers have bodies that are mortal, hearts that can be broken, spirits that need to be fed. It would be interested in experience as much as in book knowledge, and its responsibility would be the growth of whole human beings, in harmony with the planet and with one another.

The Raleigh *News and Observer* published an article a few years back reporting on a solution to the drug problem. An educator named Dr. George Busiel of Nichols Middle School in Evanston, Illinois, had started a program for children called Operation Snowflake. He said: "I think what happens to a lot of kids is that they never really learn how to handle their stress, their anger. In addition to drug education, that is

xiii

what we are trying to do, to give them some skills to handle the things that are coming up in their lives."

"To give them some skills to handle the things that are coming up in their lives" is as helpful a statement as I can imagine of the purpose of an education. It is both practical and revolutionary: practical in that instead of ignoring the strong emotions that create problems for the student, it admits them and offers help; revolutionary in that school, more often than not, has been the place that *causes* stress and anger in people's lives, instead of relieving them. A few days ago the same newspaper reported that two teenage girls in Cary, North Carolina, had committed suicide, leaving a note that apologized for bad grades and disobedience. Would an education designed to help students understand their inner turmoil have prevented this catastrophe?

I'm speaking here of an attitude toward learning that accepts the importance of the inner life. An approach to teaching that acknowledges the humanness of both teachers and students. I remember, when I try to recall, hardly any instances in which my teachers told us something about their own lives. The only instance that stands out was in third grade, when Mrs. Higgins, my favorite teacher, told us, for reasons I shall never know, that that morning her son, John, had brought her a glass of orange juice while she was in the shower. It had something to do with her having a cold. The feeling that accompanied this tiny anecdote was abundantly clear: proud pleasure. Mrs. Higgins was boasting and enjoying her boast, and I enjoyed it almost as much as she did. I saw the steamy bathroom, felt the heat and moisture in the air, saw the orange of the glass of orange juice held out toward the shower stall by the hand of the mysterious John (in my mind a tall youth with brown hair). And behind the clouded glass door was the naked body of Mrs. Higgins, enjoying itself.

What I remember thinking at the time had nothing to do with Freudian relationships. Rather, I was amazed and pleased to learn that Mrs. Higgins had a family life just as I did. I pictured her bathroom being very much like my own, her apartment another version of ours.

And her relationship to John—that was what was so interesting. I knew she had told us this little story to show us that her son cared for her, that she was loved within the bosom of her family, that she, Mrs. Higgins, despite her cold, was the luckiest person in the whole world.

I dwell on this incident because it symbolizes something that was missing from education as I knew it: the reality of private life. Taking showers, having a naked body, drinking orange juice, being a member of a family, needing to know that you are loved, needing to tell about it. It was the sense of life itself that was missing, of sensory and emotional experience not divided up into "subjects"—hygiene, psychology, nutrition, family relations—but embedded in a narrative, part of a lived history, a history I could relate to my history and the histories of the people around me, how we felt, what we really thought about, what it was like for us to be alive and going through the world.

The story about the son and the shower and the orange juice let me know that Mrs. Higgins was a human being like me, and at the same time that it made me envious (how loved she was!), it gave me hope. What the hope was founded on I can't quite say—a feeling of commonality, perhaps, a knowledge that Mrs. Higgins had needs and that her needs and mine might not be all that different.

School as I knew it taught social studies for the making of good citizens; it taught arithmetic so that we could learn how to make change, hold jobs involving computation, and pay taxes. It taught reading, writing, and spelling. But it never turned our gaze toward ourselves or each other. It never suggested that we might reach out to one another. Death was never mentioned. There was a song that accompanied a skipping game we learned in kindergarten:

> How do you do, my partner
> How do you do today?
> We will dance in a circle.
> I will show you the way.

This song brought me and my classmates face to face; it talked about how we were going to treat each other, and about how we really were. But it's a memory that has no equivalent in all my years of school.

A holistic approach to education would recognize that a person must learn how to be with other people, how to love, how to take criticism, how to grieve, how to have fun, as well as how to add and subtract, multiply and divide. It would not leave out of account that people are begotten, born, and die. It would address the need for purpose and for connectedness to ourselves and one another; it would not leave us alone to wander the world armed with plenty of knowledge but lacking the skills to handle the things that are coming up in our lives.

———

This book tells the story of how I came to view school in a radically different way. I did not set out to change my views; experience changed them for me. Some alterations in the way I taught led to greater self-consciousness about what I was doing in the classroom. This prompted me to look back into my own past as a student, to relive the school days of my childhood. As I experimented more boldly in my teaching, and delved further into the past, my inner life began to be transformed. Remembering the past was not, as I had originally thought, just an attempt to see how I had been molded as a teacher by the teachers who had molded me; it was an exploratory mission into the depths of my formation as a person, and it put me in touch for the first time with the founding experiences of my life. It helped me to discover what kind of person I had become as a result of those early school experiences, and even more, who I had been before they worked their will on me.

As memories of those old days of tribulation came back to me piecemeal, and in flashes, they put me through pains I had long forgotten. I felt and saw myself again, a child terrified that the teacher wouldn't call on her when she had to go to the Girls Room, obsessed with not making mistakes, full of the physical symptoms of distress—stomachaches, headaches, bedwetting—hating school, and not understanding why I should have to go there.

Only slowly, as the memories have ripened, have I begun to see their meanings, often so simple that I find it hard to admit their truth: such as that my school was not a healthy place for children; such as that school, although it taught me to succeed in its own terms, also stunted and misshaped me for life. The memories revealed that I had always believed school was a good place, and for a long time while writing this memoir I clung to that belief. After all, as a college professor, the fundamental rightness of school was the ground on which I'd based my existence. School was my life; it was the world. It simply never occurred to me that it might not be good at bottom.

But finally it did occur to me. The early memories woke me up to who I was—a terrified performer—and to what school had been about—obeying rules. And I gained a new perspective on the fear I felt later on as an adult experimenting in my own classroom.

I realized that the meaning of the experiments would be much clearer if set against the background of my formation as a professional literary scholar. So the middle part of the book tells how I became a professor; working hard in college and harder in graduate school—a tale of success shadowed by ignorance. By the time I'd begun to teach, I had read Dante in the original, and Virgil and Ariosto and Tasso. I knew Old English and Middle English, could read German and French, and had studied the classics of English and American literature. But my first published article, on Henry James's "The Beast in the Jungle," a story about a man whose ignorance of himself catches up with him in the end, set off an alarm. I knew this story had something important to say to me, but what? what? I couldn't tell. I was too busy, too worried about my career, and too unsure of myself to look deeply into this problem. I forged ahead. It was only much later—after many years of trying to be a good teacher and to climb the professional ladder—that I began to wake up to the rest of my life.

The last part of the book charts my struggle to make teaching a less fearful activity, the university a less intimidating place, and myself a less career-driven person. It begins with discontent with my teaching practice and an attempt to do something about it, moves to accounts of more radical experimentation during which I lost the investment I had once had in making sure students knew what I knew and what I thought, and eventually passes into existential territory where all the moorings come loose. Finally, through trying to realize my dreams of how a classroom might be, I discovered that school was not some benign and more or less permanent feature of the way life is organized but the enemy of what I wanted to learn and teach.

My experiments in teaching did not turn out to exist solely for the reasons I had given for them. I thought it was for my students' benefit that I was conducting these trials by liberation, for I saw how straitjacketed they were by the need to please and to perform for people in authority. But it wasn't only for them that I took these risks. By throwing out the window all the usual standards and structures, I was also trying to free myself from the authoritarian training that had fettered me, rebelling at all that had been done to me in the way of mind-numbing and spirit-breaking discipline. I needed to let go of the conventions that normally bind classroom behavior until I could get back to a place where there were no standard forms any longer, a time and space before school began.

In the end, my classroom experiments and the memories of P.S. 98 led me to a glimpse of the person I had been before I went to school. The search led to the parts of my self that school had sidelined or suppressed: emotion, imagination, spirituality, respect for the body's needs. I had loved the life of intellectual striving, of scholarly inquiry, challenge, and debate, but I had learned, as Arthur Koestler wrote in *Darkness at Noon*, a play I read for English class my senior year of high school, that to be guided by reason alone is sailing without ballast. I wanted to become whole. Yet more important even than the discovery of any particular part of my psyche was the recognition that there is no final source of knowledge or authority outside the self.

School, by definition, conditions us to believe that there are others who know better than we do; it encourages and often forces us to give up our own judgment in favor of the judgment of those in authority. School, by its existence, militates against the very thing that education is for—the development of the individual. This paradox is at its heart. And so, sooner or later, everyone has to leave school, if not literally, then in a spiritual sense. "There is no way set up for us," the Zen teacher Shunryū Suzuki said. "Moment after moment we have to find our own way. Some idea of perfection, or some perfect way which is set up by someone else, is not the true way for us." One must decide to let experience speak.

1

THE DREAM

OF AUTHORITY

I'm in front of the class on the first day of school, and for some reason, I'm totally unprepared. (How did this happen?) Throat tight, I fake a smile, grab for words, tell an anecdote, anything to hold their attention. But the strangers in rows in front of me aren't having any. They start to shuffle and murmur; they turn their heads away. Then chairs scrape back, and I realize it's actually happened. The students are walking out on me. I have finally gotten what I deserve.

This dream in one form or another is dreamed by thousands of teachers before the beginning of the fall semester. Some dream that they can't find their classrooms and are racing frantically through darkened halls; others that they are pontificating in nasal tones on subjects they know nothing about; others see themselves turning to write on the blackboard and feel the class leaving behind their backs. The dream is so common that most people I know discount it. "Oh, everybody has that dream," they say, dismissing the subject. But the dream is not discountable. It is about the fear of failure—the failure of one's authority—and it points to the heart of what it means to be a teacher.

When I had this dream, I'd been teaching for over fifteen years. I was a full professor at a reputable university, regarded as a good teacher and a productive scholar. So why was I having a nightmare about my students walking out on me? Where did the doubt and insecurity come from? The answer lies in another dream; in this one, I'm a student.

I am studying for my Ph.D. exams and am about to take them. Suddenly I realize I haven't studied at all. I've been doing some vague research on topics that interest me, but they aren't the right ones. I've never even cracked the surveys of English literature I'd relied on in graduate school. Why haven't I touched these books? I have twenty-five minutes before the exam. Maybe I can cram at the last minute. But instead I get myself a cup of coffee, find a good place to read, go back for my jacket, and so on, until there's no time left.

I realize then they're going to fail me. (This is all taking place at the university where I currently teach; it comes to me that this is the chance the older faculty have been waiting for to show me up for what I am.) It's a ten-hour written exam with an oral component. I've learned from a colleague I consider more learned than myself that the exam has short-answer questions such as "Who were the Fugitives?" (Do I know who the Fugitives were? I'm not sure.)

Then comes the familiar moment of recognition: I already have a Ph.D.! I decide in a frenzy of rebellion that I won't take this exam. I will not subject myself to the humiliation of failure. I'm walking up the stairs now toward the exam room; there's no time left. What will I do?

In this dream I appear as a student in an institution where I'm a full professor. I'm almost fifty, dreaming of being in the position of a twenty-four-year-old. Here, as in the other dream, I'm a fraud, someone who's supposed to know things she doesn't actually know. It's the same situation, really; only this time instead of being humiliated and rejected by students, I'm going to be humiliated and rejected by teachers, people in authority over me. The old fear, the exam fear, never goes away. As you go through life, it just gets projected onto other situations. If you become a teacher, the fear is projected onto your students. They don't

2

have the power over you that your teachers once had, but your internalized fear gives them the power.

Terror is like a ball that bounces back and forth between two walls of a small room. Once you throw it hard at one wall, it rebounds to the other and then back against the first, and so on until it loses momentum and gravity pulls it to the floor. With terror, though, I'm not sure what stops the ball, or whether in some instances it doesn't pick up speed and bounce harder. The walls in this metaphor are teachers and students, and the ball is the fear they pass back and forth.

Looking back, I now see that because of these fears, I developed, over the years, a good-cop/bad-cop routine in the classroom. In order to win my students' love, I would try to divest myself of authority by constant self-questioning, by deference to students' opinions; through disarming self-revelation, flattery, jokes, criticizing school authorities; by accepting late papers, late attendance, and nonperformance of various kinds. Meanwhile, in order to establish and maintain my authority, I would almost invariably come to class overprepared, allowing no deviations from the plan for the day, making everything I said as complex, high level, and idiosyncratic as possible lest the students think I wasn't as smart as they were. I would pile on the work, grade hard, and—this must have confused them—tell them that all I cared about was their individual development.

It's easy, though, to caricature the devices I'd stoop to in order to both yield and keep hold of authority. It's easy to criticize. If I alternately intimidated and placated the students it's because I was threatened and felt afraid, afraid of my students, and afraid of the authorities who had stood in judgment on me long ago.

The image of authority is embodied for me in teachers. Mrs. Colgan in 1B, standing tense and straight in a black dress with little white spots that droops on her figure. Her lips are pursed, her hair is in a hairnet, her black eyes snap with intensity, and her whole thin being radiates the

3

righteous authority she exercises over us; it is mixed with wrath. She is scolding, holding a small book in front of her flat, draped chest. Mrs. Colgan has to exert all the energy she has to maintain this stance. Most of the time she spoke to us in a soft, gentle voice; she liked to be soft and gentle with the children. Only when someone really stepped out of line did she become her steely, purse-lipped self. Because I saw this, I was only afraid of Mrs. Colgan, not terrified of her. I saw in her the two faces of authority: the desire to lead gently, to be kind and affectionate, to love; and the necessity to instill fear, the desperation of having to beat back the enemy by whatever means.

It's the second image that tends to remain in people's memories. The teacher, the one who stands in front, who stands while others sit, the one whom you must obey, the one who exacts obedience. For obedience is the basis for everything else that happens in school; unless the children obey, nothing can be taught. That is what I learned. Obedience first. Or rather, fear first, fear of authority, yielding obedience, then, everything else.

There was a boy in the second or third grade who symbolized the need for the kind of authority I hated. I'll call him Louis Koslowski. He was always bad. Nothing the teachers could do or say ever shut Louis up. He could be temporarily quelled, but sooner or later he always came back for more. I was terrified of being spoken to and about the way the teachers spoke to and about Louis Koslowski, for he brought out the worst in them: shouting, name-calling, intimidation; every form of sarcasm and ridicule they could command, every threat, every device of shaming. If there had been stocks in P.S. 98, Louis Koslowski would have been in them.

Louis, though, like Mrs. Colgan, had two sides. He was terrible, we were told; he was the universal troublemaker without whom everything would have been fine. And surely he caused us to suffer through hours of yelling, and hours of leftover bad feeling spilling over from the teacher onto us, and oozing out from us into the corners of the room. But he was cute, his energy was exciting; he was an appealing figure in a rough-and-tumble way. Sometimes I thought the teachers were right, but sometimes I thought he was being picked on unfairly. Why make such a fuss? I mean, we were supposed to sit all day, hands folded on our desks, legs crossed (if you were a girl), silent, staring forward in our rows. Looking back on it now, it seems that much of the time in school, the only interest or action lay in the power struggle between the teachers, whose reign of terror enforced the rules, and the students like Louis K., whose irrepressible energy contested them.

But the struggle was not for me.

I have another image of a boy in third grade—his name was Steven Kirschner—a pretty blond child with sky blue eyes and a soft-as-doeskin nature. He is standing at attention next to his seat, being dressed down by the teacher for some slight. I don't remember what it was, but I knew he didn't deserve such treatment. He stands there, stiffly, hands at his sides, in brown corduroy pants. His china blue eyes brim with the tears he's trying to hold back. He is the very picture of innocence abused, yet the lash, metaphorically, fell on him just the same. And it fell on me, too, for strange as it may seem, I did not distinguish between myself and the unhappy scapegoat for the teacher's wrath. And so when Mrs. Garrity, the worst one of all, with her brown suit and red face made red by perennial anger, was heard screaming horribly and interminably in the hall at some unlucky person, it seemed to me entirely an accident that that person had not yet been me; when Mrs. Seebach, of the enormous bosom and enormous behind, bellowed at us in gym class, seized by demonic rage over a student's failure properly to execute grand right and left, I trembled. I could have made the same mistake. Once Mrs. Seebach did ridicule me in front of the class because I didn't know how to tie a knot at the end of a piece of thread; there was no knowing when it would happen again.

It was executioner and victim in my scenario, and the victims had better watch out. For above these harridans were other authorities even more august. Mr. Rothman, the new principal, and (holy of holies) Mr. Zimmerman, superintendent of schools: presences so terrible no one dared, not even the Louis Koslowskis, to so much as breathe naturally as we stood in rigid rows for their inspection. When I look back on my early years in school, it's Steven Kirschner standing helpless next to his desk whom I identify with, not Louis Koslowski rolling a spitball under his, and certainly not with the teachers.

You would think that with experiences like these so vivid in my mind, I would have avoided school, but no. I became a teacher. I *joined*. The teachers I consciously modelled myself on were not the ones I've been describing but teachers I had later in junior high and high school, teachers who never used the metaphoric whip, but inspired, encouraged, and praised. Still, the older models remain; the deeper stratum lies underneath, its breath of ancient terror haunting me. Unless I perform for the authorities, unless I do what I'm told, I will be publicly shamed.

My own early and repeated exposure to authorities who terrified me absolutely helps to explain my habit of alternate rebellion against and submission to the authority figures in my life. And it accounts at least in part for my contradictory behavior toward my students: wanting to control and not to control, wanting to be loved—and obeyed.

The pedagogy that produces oppression starts early and comes from traditions of childrearing like those Alice Miller describes in *For Your Own Good*, where she writes: "Child-rearing is basically directed not toward the *child's* welfare but toward satisfying the parents' need for power and revenge." This need, in its turn, is created by abuse suffered and forgotten. "It is precisely those events that have never been come to terms with that must seek an outlet," says Miller. "The jubilation characteristic of those who declare war is the expression of the revived hope of finally being able to avenge earlier debasement, and presumably also of relief at finally being permitted to hate and shout."

I do not know what earlier debasements the teachers at P.S. 98 were avenging when they screamed at us in the halls, but I know they must

6

have been the object of someone's vengefulness. Their hatred and shouting are still echoing in my mind, and I'm sure I cannot be the only one.

Eventually, I became aware that childhood experiences of authority had controlled, without my knowing it, the way I exercised and failed to exercise authority as an adult, and that it was the reality of what had happened at P.S. 98, more than my present one, that had been dictating the terms of my university life, day to day. Fear was the underside of that life. Much of my behavior had been ruled by it. The fear stayed buried, controlling me secretly, because, though I became learned, was taught four languages, three literatures, and many other things beside, I'd not been taught how to recognize and face my fear. Learning this for myself has been frightening and discouraging and a long study. But for me, it seems, there was no other way.

2

P.S. 98

For a long time part of me has wanted to revisit the dark corridors of P.S. 98, to stand there listening to the anger in the teachers' voices. The reason it's taken me this long is that a voice inside me gets in the way. *You don't have a story to tell*, it says. *Whatever you felt wasn't that bad. And even if it was, complaining about it is childish. After all, most people experience the same things, or worse.*

Who do you think you are? the voice says. *Just who do you think you are?*

When I start to write and the voice makes belittling remarks, I put it off on others. I say, this is my mother's voice, the voice of authority, of people who had it worse than I did and can't stand to hear me suffer out loud. But it's not really their voice anymore. It's mine. I speak that language of derision. I have had to struggle to get by this censorious person, who would shut me up if she could.

To begin at the beginning, I didn't want to get up in the morning.

Who does? What's the big deal?

Look, *I'm* telling this, not you. It was important that I didn't want to get up, because the reason was, I was afraid of school.

8

Most mornings I was pulled from sleep by my father, whose kind presence shielded me, temporarily, from what I knew I had to face. Right away, the feelings in my stomach began. Butterflies, nausea, hollowness, nagging pain, sharp pain: my repertoire. Which one I felt would depend on what I was worried about that day. I lit the lamp on my bureau. I dressed.

In TV commercials, when people wake up in the morning the sun comes streaming in their windows, falling lavishly on their bedclothes, spilling onto the floor. The atmosphere is bathed in joyous light. The air is dancing. Who wouldn't want to wake up under such conditions? When I got up, it was dark. It's usually dark inside houses in the morning, and cold, too. What matters, though, is not the dark or the cold, but the spirit of the waker. This is where the bodies are buried. You want to know what's going on in someone's life? Ask them how they feel first thing in the morning.

So there I am standing in front of my mirror, a large clear mirror in a wooden frame that hangs over my dresser, trying to figure out what's wrong. I feel sick, only I'm not sick. I just feel bad inside. I know there's something wrong with me, but what? The sickness is not the stomachache; it's something about me.

Looking in the mirror, I see a blonde girl, on the skinny side, blue eyes, high forehead. Nice-looking. But it's not the outward things that matter. Something's the matter with me on the inside; it's as if I smelled bad.

My clothes aren't right either. Do you understand? My clothes are perfectly fine, but to me they're not. Oh, they look all right while I'm at home, but when I get to school I see how the other girls dress, how they know what to do with hair ribbons, and how their blouses are tucked in just right. They have a mysterious knowledge of the world; they know everything. How to giggle at the right time. Not me. I stand or sit there, taking it all in, solemnly watching. I know this because people would accuse: "Why are you so *serious*?" they'd say. In fact, I wasn't serious. I was just nonplussed and scared. My reactions weren't the same as the other kids'. What they did didn't come naturally to me. I was different.

Different? Everybody thinks they're different.

Well, I *was.* Not as different as I thought, maybe, but some. Because I had no brothers or sisters (everybody I knew did), because I was neither Jewish nor Catholic (everybody I knew was), because I wanted so badly to obey the rules (most of the other kids seemed not to think rules were important), because my stomach was filled with fear (who knew what was going on inside other people's stomachs?), because my father wore a brown suit, because my mother took naps in the afternoon, because . . . Who knows why? It's how I felt.

My father would make breakfast, and we'd sit at the little table in the corner of the kitchen with the window looking onto the grey courtyard. I wished breakfast could last forever. On Saturday mornings we'd sit for long hours, and my father would tell stories over the eggs and toast: the "How I Used to Work for Santa Claus" series, and the Charles Googenwart stories about a bad boy who went to a school like mine and got away with murder. He even outwitted the President of the Board of Education! I loved these stories and savored every minute. That was on the weekend.

But on weekdays as we'd sit there, the seconds and minutes would be unwinding, unwinding, and my mind would dart desperately around for something to hold on to that would keep us there, safe. If my stomachache was bad, I'd whimper that I didn't want to go to school. Sometimes he'd take me in his lap to comfort me, and I'd put my arms around his neck and feel the pain in my stomach. I thought it an outrage to have to go to school *and* have a stomachache at the same time. Sometimes my mother would get up and come to the living room in her bathrobe and try to talk to me; they were worried, I knew. But there was nothing to be done—though *why* there was nothing to be done, I couldn't understand. I had to go to school, stomachache or no stomachache. Out of the dark apartment. Down the dark stairs, onto the glaring sidewalk, the world.

If I took the bus, I waited on the sidewalk next to the maroon awning over the main entrance to our building. I stared at the dark brick of the building across the street and at the vacant lot next to it. There were other kids at the bus stop, but I don't remember them.

In cold weather, if I was lucky, I would be wearing kneesocks—not the babyish snowsuit or leggings my mother preferred. I'd feel the cold on the smooth skin on the inside of my knees where they touched, pink from the cold air, proud emblem of being grown-up. On winter mornings I would read the thermometer, run to my mother's bedroom and say: "Forty degrees, Mamma, forty degrees," heart in my mouth. That was the cutoff, the line between leggings or no leggings. A couple of times I lied to avoid the snowsuit, and got found out. But only once or twice; my mother's disapproval so stern it wasn't worth risking. "Jane, you *know* . . ." and then a look of stern reproof. That was enough.

Finally the bus would come roaring down the cobblestone hill, the door would fold open with a shriek, and there would be Joey, the bus driver. A froglike man in face and figure, sallow skin and dark uniform, he was loud-mouthed and good-natured and always cracking the same old wisecracks. Joey didn't hate the kids. He yapped when they got too rambunctious, but he never meant anything bad. The kids were forever making too much noise. Life was no picnic, but . . . If everybody in the world had been like Joey, things wouldn't have been so bad.

Bad?

Look, I know from the outside this doesn't look so bad. I know I lived in a nice middle-class home. I know I had all the advantages. I know my parents loved me. But that makes it worse, don't you see? If I had anything real to complain about, beatings, mistreatment, neglect, it would be easier. The way it is, all the unhappiness seems to be my responsibility, my fault.

I was glad when the bus arrived, the orange yellow box filled with eventfulness. But as soon as I got on, I was sorry. The dark interior with its shiny seats, and noisy children, confused me. What were they shouting at? How did they dare? Lots of them seemed to know each other, but did they? It was hard to tell, they were so uproarious, bouncing up and down, throwing things, yelling. I sat still, afraid of being reprimanded even by the good-natured Joey, because, who knew? He could always catch me for disobeying some rule I hadn't guessed. School, and everything associated with it, was founded on rules, and I learned that I could never know them all or manage to obey perfectly the ones I did know.

It was lonely on the bus, where I felt my difference from the bouncing, bellowing children, lonely in another way when I walked. One particular morning I walked with my father down Seaman Avenue, he on the way to the subway, I on the way to school. He was wearing the brown suit I loathed, the one that made me embarrassed to be seen with him, though I loved my father and was comforted by his presence next to me. As I walked along the wall that divided Seaman Avenue from Inwood Park, my hand in his, my stomach was filled with waves of panic. This walk would be over soon. Soon I would have to let go of his hand and go on by myself to school. Since it was fall, occasionally I skipped around trying to step on leaves to feel them crunch and hear them crackle beneath my shoe. Then another wave would sweep through me and I would return to my father's hand. The knowledge that after we reached the subway at 211th and Broadway everything would change put a barrier between us. He loved me, I knew, but he could do nothing for me. The walk, though companionable, was painful because it reminded me that soon I would have to be alone, and so would he. We were bound to our separate fates.

On days when I walked to school I left early so that I would never, ever be picked on for not being there on time, never be caught not knowing what I was supposed to do because I'd arrived too late to hear the command. My parents used to joke that I got to school before the janitor. But I didn't care; *anything* was better than being late. It would have meant being singled out by a teacher, screamed at in front of everybody, the way other kids were, humiliated in front of the whole school. I knew I couldn't stand it if that were to happen to me.

The trouble with getting there early was, I had to wait in the schoolyard, a place completely barren, surrounded on three sides by high brick walls, and covered in aged concrete. No matter what the season, it was always dark and cold in the morning shadow. It made my stomach worse. On one side, stairs led up to three sets of doors, all locked. At first the wait in the vacant yard seemed endless, but suddenly the yard would fill up until it boiled with children, shouting, running, pushing, twirling, moping. From emptiness, it was chaos in a second. I waited them both out, like a sentinel on duty, withdrawn, until a sharp whistle brought us to attention. Long lines formed facing the school building; exhortations to silence and immobility from the monitor. We stood stock-still and quiet, though never quiet or still enough for her. We waited and waited. Finally the order was given, and in we filed.

We surged up the dark stairwells, making the iron steps rumble. Stalled by mysterious traffic jams, we stood on the dark stairs in our winter coats, breathing, awaiting the pleasure of the safety patrols, older students who stood on the landings directing traffic. They imitated the tactics of the teachers, shouting and threatening awful things to people who walked on the wrong side, talked, or otherwise got out of line. They could get you for anything: making a noise, chewing gum, just *looking* wrong. I was picked on simply for being scared—"BIG EYES! Whatsa matter with you? Huh?"

After the boxcar conditions of yard and stairs, the classroom, for a few minutes, was a safe haven. It would be light and warm in there; the faces and the ground rules familiar. Pretty soon, though, something would

13

trigger my anxieties, and I would have to go to the bathroom. And so would begin the cycle of fear and release from fear that was the burden of my days in school.

Having to go to the bathroom so often was in itself a source of anxiety. I lived in terror of wetting my pants in front of the whole class, and finally did while I was giving a book report in sixth grade. I worried constantly that the teacher wouldn't recognize me when I raised my hand, or wouldn't let me go when I asked permission. In one class, my mother made a special arrangement with the teacher that I could go to the Girls Room whenever I wanted, and after that I felt less nervous, though the arrangement itself was a source of shame.

When I got to the Girls Room, overjoyed that I hadn't wet my pants, going to the bathroom after holding it in for so long felt like heaven. Besides, the Girls Room was a respite from the inquisition of the classroom. It had a row of dark green stalls on the left, sinks and mirrors on the right that reflected the light, a floor of white octagonal tiles, and at the far end, a dirty window. There was no privacy unless you wanted to keep company with a toilet, but it was nice to be out of the public gaze even for a moment. I dreamt once that I had come to school in my cotton underwear and was trying to hide by crawling among the dusty pipes that ran above the stalls.

It's not only the Girls Room at P.S. 98 I remember in such detail. All the rooms—the library, the principal's office, the auditorium, the basement, every classroom I ever had, even a supply closet where an intelligence test was once administered to me by a graduate student—are there today at my beck and call. The best room, the one with the fewest unpleasant memories, was kindergarten. Though the basic fact of kindergarten was that I felt like an orphan, there were times when I was happy. The room was a light-filled space, with big windows down one side, little chairs, and cubbies where we put our things. I think if I could have stayed there longer, getting used to school, it might have been easier for me later on.

The teachers, Miss Morget (pronounced *mor-zhay*) and Miss Hunt, were tall and thin but unalike in every other way. Miss Hunt was young and attractive. She had chestnut brown hair, stylishly rolled, hazel eyes, and a prominent chin. At first, her smart outfits and polished good looks fooled me into thinking she was the nice one. But there was a twist to her mouth sometimes and a troubled look in her eyes that frightened me, and when she spoke to the children, there was iron in her voice. Miss Morget was old and kind. Her frizzled white hair stuck out, softening her sharp nose; and her pale eyes, which held a twinkle, made me pretty sure she wasn't going to do or say anything mean. She spoke in a gentle, cracked voice that was never angry; but the children knew when she meant business, and they minded.

In kindergarten we sat in a circle for cookies and milk, which I liked; lay down on mats for naptime, which I hated; painted pictures and glued things together, which I could take or leave; and played dancing and singing games, which I loved. That was when the fun began. We pushed our chairs back to make a space, the teacher put a record on, or played the piano, and for a little while that piece of linoleum floor where we skipped in time to the music was the place I wanted to be. We held hands, stood in a circle, marched around to music, bowing, curtsying, making motions or noises to match the words of the song: "Go in and out the Window," "London Bridge Is Falling Down," "Old MacDonald Had a Farm," "The Farmer in the Dell," "A Tisket a Tasket," and best of all, "How Do You Do, My Partner."

The girls would curtsy, and the boys would bow. (Steven Kirschner in a V-neck sweater places an arm across his waist, and the top of his head comes into view as he lowers it stiffly in my direction.) Then we'd take hands and skip around the circle two by two. It didn't matter if your partner was a boy or a girl; it was the coziest, friendliest, most comforting thing to do. The formality of curtsy and bow, the joining of hands—both hands—the skipping in tandem, a little out of step, made kindergarten and the whole world feel safe. My partner, how do you do? We will dance. I will show you. . . . I never wanted it to be over.

———

First grade with Miss Toy, right next to the kindergarten room, put an end to that. We sat in rows and had to keep our mouths zipped shut, backs straight, hands folded in our laps. Joanne Jones, whose cotton skirts and blouses were always ironed to perfection, was praised for sitting with her legs crossed. "Very nice and ladylike," said Miss Toy. Joanne looked happy and composed, as if she liked to sit that way. I hastily pretended that I liked to, too, though it didn't make sense. In school, I thought, the thing was to be smart. But what was this about being ladylike? Miss Toy seemed to regard it as some kind of accomplishment. Impatiently I thought, Let's get on with reading.

Reading, in 1A, meant flashcards. The teacher stood in front of the room holding a bunch of cards and flashed them at us one at a time. She would call on someone to read the word and then go on to the next card. I liked this game, which wasn't as boring as it could have been since Miss Toy kept up a good pace, and I liked it especially when anybody could call out the answer, for I knew all the words and was desperate to show off my knowledge. Sitting there in the fourth seat of the second row, embarked now upon the grand adventure of first grade, I yearned for recognition. Here I am, I cried inwardly. Here I am! See me! Here we all are, raring to go, dying to be off on the great voyage of exploration. Yet strangely, there we sat, day after day, still in the same rows. And all our wild blood and huge desires were funnelled into what pleased Miss Toy the most: sitting with backs straight, eyes straight ahead, hands folded in laps.

Miss Toy's was a Spartan regime, though not the worst. She was a brisk, no-nonsense person who dropped no stitches and suffered none to be dropped. Everything feathery and diaphanous had been clipped from her character long ago, and now her baleful expression served as a reminder that business was business. Miss Toy was fair and never treated anyone very badly, but in her class there was a chill in the air, and the possibility of being nicked by a dry, sharp tongue.

With this instrument, we were kept in line, and because it was all so new—the flashcards, the blackboards, sitting in rows—hope staggered on. In 1B, the second half of first grade, that hope suffered a near-fatal blow.

I am sitting in the second or third seat of the row nearest the door. There are six or seven rows, each with eight or nine seats. We are learning to read. The drill is this: We start with the row nearest the window, or with the row nearest the door, and one by one, up and down the rows, each student reads aloud a few lines of Dick and Jane. "Dick said, 'See Spot run! See Spot run, Jane!' " Student after student stumbles and halts painfully over simple words. I strain with the strainers, stutter with the stutterers, but finally I give up. It is too painful. The Dick and Jane books are an insult; they are so unreal, they are incomprehensible. And here we are, going over the story one more time—though there *is* no story, just statements that no one would ever make about people who never existed. I can't believe that this is all there is to reading. Where is the world? Where is excitement and discovery? But after a while I do believe it.

I had wanted to read so badly that I had made my mother teach me some fundamentals while I was still in kindergarten. I'd been so disappointed when I got to school and found out we weren't going to read that year. What else did you go to school for? I got some blue books from Miss Morget, but all she would do was let me copy things over in them. I couldn't see any point in that, so I got my mother to teach me. I pestered her.

17

By the time I got to 1B not only could I already read, but I could read books much more complicated than Dick and Jane, which I would have read from cover to cover in the first five minutes of the day we got them. Besides, it was the *way* reading was taught that made it so boring: everybody listening while the slowest student stumbled and stuttered; everything uniform and predictable; up and down the endless rows, day after day.

That was reading, and the other subjects were pretty much the same. Penmanship. A great big A with a little *a* next to it. A great big B with a little *b* next to it. A great big C with a little *c* next to it. These we copied diligently into our notebooks. *D,d,E,e, ...*

What I expected from school and what I got were different beyond belief. Though I never completely gave up hoping the two would coincide, something happened to my sense of possibility there that cramped it permanently. I didn't know it was happening; it didn't happen all at once; and I couldn't have told you what it was exactly that was going on. But as what I experienced clashed absolutely with my inward expectations and desires, the shape of any future desire or expectation I might have was forever blunted.

At P.S. 98 the three basics were not reading, writing, and arithmetic but standing in line, not moving, and staying absolutely quiet. These seemed to be what all of the teachers, the principal, the superintendent of schools, and all other figures of authority were most impressed by. I spent a good deal of time wondering by what error this had come to pass. I thought school was supposed to be a place where you learned things, but it seemed that I spent hours standing in dark corridors waiting for commands to be given and listening to the teachers bellow out their rage at students who weren't standing there just right.

School, I had thought, was to be a voyage of discovery, an expedition into the mountainous world of adults, full of tortuous paths, perilous peaks, sudden gorges, magnificent vistas. This journey would require

18

everything I had but would be worth it, for in the end, I would get to see what adults saw: the great world itself. I yearned for a glimpse of this panorama. I wanted to see it spread out before me, all at once.

At P.S. 98 the great world came to us in the form of *My Weekly Reader*, a newspaper on current events devised specifically for schoolchildren and offered to us with considerable fanfare as a treat. I found it so tasteless and dry that I thought there must be something the matter with me. If it was so special, why didn't I like it? I couldn't tell, but dutifully I forced it down. In itself, *My Weekly Reader* was nothing, just a minor letdown. But it stood for an enforced fraudulence that crept into so many things we did.

On a regular basis we were sent to the auditorium to learn songs from Mrs. Rothman, a middle-aged woman with round glasses, dark hair, and coarse skin. With great perseverance she taught us the words to songs that had no possible relationship to our lives. One I particularly hated ended with the words

> In my grandma's garden, a robin sings tweet tweet tweet tweet.
> At a bright early hour, he wakens each flower,
> Just singing to grandma and me.

I had no living grandparents, knew no one with a garden, and hated to get up early. But what really made me hate this song was the niceness of it and the way Mrs. Rothman seemed to imply that such sugary experiences should be a familiar part of all our lives.

There was something maddeningly contrived about those songs. In their way, they were like the *Weekly Reader*. You could tell that the subject had been chosen for children and then treated in a way that "children" could understand. It was the condescension, so obvious and humiliating, that got to me. The songs were harmless, I suppose, and learning them was certainly preferable to sitting in class. But as I write about them now, an old feeling of bitterness rises in my throat. Why, out of all the millions of songs, did we have to sing those? I preferred the song the policemen who came every year and told the same jokes taught us: "Remember your name and address." At least it made practical sense.

———

Once a week, at around three fifteen, we had Camp Fire Girls. We met in the basement, a place of pipes and posts, of discarded desks and furnace smells and darkness. I went there because of the words: Camp Fire Girls! Flames leaping in the forest night, wilderness, adventure! A company of the intrepid, the fearless, those who would dare and do! I used to wonder what the things we did in that basement had to do with the images Camp Fire Girls aroused in me, and I kept waiting for the day when the veil would be withdrawn. For surely what was in store for us had to be more exciting than what we were doing: making pictures using a toothbrush dipped in paint, rubbing it over a piece of screen so that the paint splattered onto a piece of colored paper on which a leaf had been placed. Surely this was only a temporary measure and would soon give way to startling adventure.

But the instructor, Miss Ann, an older woman with a soft voice, wispy hair and an atmosphere of disappointment, did not seem promising. The bristles of the toothbrush she brought to do her screen painting with were pink, and I knew that that meant she had bleeding gums, which was a bad sign. All in all, Miss Ann, who never raised her voice above a whisper, did not seem a likely candidate for leading brave girls on risky expeditions. It was some time before I believed that the basement and Miss Ann and her make-work tasks were all that would be forthcoming. And I continued to suppose that somewhere were the real Camp Fire Girls, doing the things that Camp Fire Girls, the true ones, really did. The disappointments of singing and Camp Fire Girls were not in themselves crushing; rather they leached away the hope that had been placed in them because the central business of school was already dead.

Repetition was the means of execution. Paying attention to what was going on in class was like being hit on the head with a wooden mallet over and over again. Maybe the teachers thought we couldn't learn anything unless it was repeated two, three, four times. For example, there was the little book about how Peter Minuit bought Manhattan Island from the Indians for twenty-four dollars and some glass beads, the only new book our class ever had. We read it over and over, and each time it was presented as if we had never seen it before. What did they think, that we had amnesia?

Sometimes it seemed to me that there gaped an enormous chasm between pupils and teachers, that the teachers, perhaps through no fault of their own, simply didn't know what was going on inside our heads. It was as if they didn't know who we were. Otherwise, how could they treat us this way? Or, it would occur to me, painfully, that what was going on inside *other* students' heads was different from what was going on inside mine, and that perhaps they really needed the repetition, the yelling, the threats, the sitting still. But it seemed unlikely. All I knew for sure was that as far as I was concerned, nearly everything the teachers did was either a mystery or a mistake. Why? Why? But though I longed to know the reason for the endless repetition we were subjected to in the course of learning anything, it never occurred to me to question that other hated feature of the way we were taught at P.S. 98, namely, the tests.

I didn't recognize tests as a teaching device. They were more like a permanent feature of the landscape, like the desks and blackboards. All I cared about was their effect—which was to frighten me. Failing a test, or getting several answers wrong, or even *one* answer wrong, was a humiliation I couldn't bear.

There was the thin beige paper with numbers I had carefully pencilled in and big red check marks next to each problem (a check meant "correct" at P.S. 98, though at other schools, I found out, it could mean

21

"wrong"). My goal in life was a paper with all red checks, not because I wanted the praise so much (though I did), and not because I wanted to be the best in the class (though I wanted that, too). These were mere side consequences of the main aim, which was to avoid disapproval. I couldn't stand to be criticized or found wanting in anything by my teachers. It didn't matter how many times I got 100 on my tests; I never believed in my ability to do it again. As far as I was concerned, I could fail at any time.

One day in 2A, Mrs. Cohen was grading our arithmetic quizzes. Mrs. Cohen had a big nose, a deep voice, and an upsweep. She wore patterned smocks over her clothes. Though at some level I knew she meant well, she scared me to death with her booming voice and her insistent threat that we were going to get *organized*. If only I had known what that word meant. We stood on line across the front and down the side of the room, waiting to approach her desk. When you got there she'd glance quickly at your test and then tell you to stand at a particular place in the room according to how well you'd done. Me she sent to stand in a corner by myself. Because it was a corner, I figured I might be the dunce, so I turned and pretended to look at some pictures on the wall. That way, if I were being punished for getting a poor grade, I'd be facing the wall, and if not, I was just looking at pictures. I'd been standing in the corner for some time when Mrs. Cohen spotted me. Her voice boomed out: "Jane, did you think I sent you to that corner for punishment?" I trembled. It was hard to escape shame no matter what you did. It turned out that I had gotten the highest mark in the class, but somehow I hadn't managed to intuit the system by which we were being posted around the room, so I managed to call down unfavorable attention on myself anyway.

To me, this was what school was really about—avoiding shame. If you were a good person, you got a perfect score on your tests. If you were a bad person, you made a lot of mistakes. Good people were praised, and bad people were humiliated. This was the true content of what we learned.

One day in third grade we were grading our own tests. The teacher read the answers aloud, and we made our own checks on the paper—or X's if we'd gotten one wrong. Sure enough, I had. But before the papers were collected came a portentous announcement. "Everyone who got number three wrong, stand up!" Lots of people stood, but not me. I'd gotten it wrong, but since we'd graded our own tests, who'd be the wiser? The next thing I knew, I heard words explaining that there had been a *mistake* in the reading of the answers. The correct answer was the one I had written down after all! Hoping no one would notice, I slowly slid to a stand, catching a glimpse of Phyllis Hantman doing the same thing out of the corner of my eye. (Her mother taught fifth grade.) We were caught and made an example of.

Phyllis and I were ashamed to admit publicly that we had gotten an answer wrong. Though I hated to lie and believed that doing so was bad, getting an answer wrong was even worse. Of course, it never occurred to us that we could have gotten the answer right when the teacher said otherwise, for we had learned that authority was always right, even when it didn't seem that way. We had learned to add and subtract at P.S. 98 and to multiply and divide. We had learned to read and write and had picked up some pretty dull information. But more than anything we had learned that we must avoid reproach and obtain approval. That was what motivated us to get our answers right, not the thirst for knowledge that had possessed us before we entered school.

———

I was so sensitive to the wishes of my teachers that I became, very early on, a teacher's pet. This happened in 1B or 2A, when I started to be monitor.

The monitor, in case you don't know, is the pupil the teacher picks to be in charge when she has to leave the room. The monitor stands in front of the class and watches. When someone misbehaves—talks, throws something, starts a fight, makes noise—she writes that person's name on the blackboard, on the Bad List. On the Good List go the names of people who sit nice as pie, backs straight, legs crossed, hands folded in their laps.

I was proud to be monitor. When the teacher chose me to take her place, I felt important and excited; the mantle of authority had descended on my shoulders, and I rose, eager to wear it. This didn't last. When I got to the front of the room I would hover in the space between the desks and the blackboard—which felt enormous—uncertain what to do. If nothing happened I felt stupid just standing there, chalk in hand. If something did happen, little spurts of unease shot through me as I wrote down the names of malefactors. I had an obscure feeling that there might be something wrong with this, but the conflict never defined itself. Dutifully I wrote *B* for Bad, *G* for Good—and wrote people's initials underneath—S.K., P.S.—sometimes erasing them and substituting different ones, according to how the drama unfolded and respecting the opinions of the class. For sometimes it would be pointed out who should go on which list, and arguments would even break out over whether somebody deserved to be on a given list or not. So when the teacher got back I was relieved, happy to give over the burden of judgment to her, though the next time, I'd never remember what it had been like, so I would rise again, eager to play my part.

The bait was attention and approval. Attention from my classmates, approval from the teacher. It was hard to get approval from both at the same time. But I was so obtuse where other children were concerned, and so eager to please the teacher, that I constantly sacrificed my chance of solidarity with the class for her good opinion.

24

My friend Jan asks: If what you're saying about school is true, where did the emotion and enthusiasm of your scholarly work come from? Aren't you leaving something out?

Probably. For a long time I've wondered why my memories of childhood are so negative. I never thought of myself as an unhappy child, yet almost everything I remember is painful. It's as if I had to acknowledge the unhappy memories I'd been storing up all these years before I could get to the good ones. But why are the good feelings so long in coming? Perhaps a mental habit of looking at things negatively, which I have recently recognized as coloring my perceptions of events, shadows my past as well. Perhaps until I clear out whatever is making me see darkly now, I won't be able to see the light that shone then.

———

The light coming through the classroom windows in third and fourth grade, when I had Mrs. Higgins, was brighter than in any of the other classrooms I'd been in except kindergarten. Her room was in a corner of the building and had windows on two sides. I sat in the third seat of the third row from the door, right in the middle of the class and slightly toward the front, protected by the other children around me, and close to the teacher, but not too close. When I locate myself there, in front of Erica Kramer and next to Peter Strauss, I feel comfortable, safe in the knowledge that nothing too terrible was likely to happen to me while sitting in that seat.

I was sitting in my seat in 2A, cowed, as usual, under Mrs. Cohen's stern regime, on the day that we first discovered that Mrs. Higgins was to be our teacher. Into the class she came—Rose Higgins! I loved even her name. She walked up and down the side of the classroom where the cloakroom was (Mrs. Cohen never went there), and called us her darlings. We were going to be in Mrs. Higgins's class, the nicest teacher in the school. All the kids wanted her.

What I loved about her most was her physical appearance. That day she came into second grade, was she wearing her white cable-knit sweater, so soft and fine, the sleeves pushed up, her arms folded under her bosom, her polished fingernails peeking out from the folds of the sleeves, the point of her pencil pointed away so she wouldn't mar her clothes, and the bangle on her bracelet dangling down?

It was as though she dressed and groomed and primped for all of us. I can see her applying powder to her nose, bending her knees slightly so that she can see her reflection in the mirror, patting her hair, brushing off her shoulders and chest lightly with her hand. I see her in her navy blue-and-white houndstooth woolen skirt, the kind that when you whirl around it lifts gracefully, with a matching navy blue fitted jacket that she pulled down into place in a little routine grooming gesture that I loved. I can see the creamy softness of her white blouse and her snappy navy blue pumps, and how she pivoted around on them as if they were dancing shoes. Sometimes she almost pranced in front of us, a combination of matronly softness, amplitude, and style.

I note this because even then, in third grade, I possessed the notion that clothes and hair and grooming weren't supposed to be important. They had to be *right*, of course, but you didn't delight in them for their own sake the way Mrs. Higgins obviously did. School was supposed to be about arithmetic and reading, not about bodies, lipstick, rouge, and navy blue leather pumps. Yet in Mrs. Higgins's class, on its best days, the feeling was Rose Higgins is in her navy blue outfit, and all's right with the world.

The other reason I loved Mrs. Higgins was that she spoke to us kindly. I knew that sometimes she was buttering us up, but that was all right. Sometimes the school principal would come in, or someone in authority, and Mrs. Higgins would have us sit very straight in our seats, eyes looking straight ahead, and she would beam at us and call us her chickadees and tell the principal or the stranger how wonderful we were. I always suspected these performances but loved them just the same. I was proud to be in Mrs. Higgins's class, and lucky, lucky to have her crowing over us. The light would reflect off her glasses (Mrs. Higgins wore glasses, though not all the time), and we would bask and sit even straighter in the light of her praise.

Mrs. Higgins's bland good nature gave the course of our days a smooth consistency, day following day like servings of cream of wheat: mild and monotonous. I think we didn't learn very much from her (when Mrs. Hantman, the fifth-grade teacher, got us, she was shocked at how little we knew), but she didn't shout at us. She treated us nicely. She made us feel it was a privilege to be who and where we were—her children, the children in her third-grade class—and though nothing special ever happened while we were there, we knew that we would be safe from the terrible rantings and ravings we heard other teachers dealing out in the halls.

Good things happened sometimes in Mrs. Higgins's class. For instance, choral speaking. There was to be a contest in the auditorium to determine which class could best speak a poem aloud in unison. We practiced for weeks. Our class did A. A. Milne's "James James Morrison Morrison Wetherby George Dupree," which I considered babyish, especially since the fifth grade was doing a poem about Columbus ("Sail on, sail on, sail on and on!"), which seemed exciting and grown-up by comparison. Still, I loved practicing our poem.

We stood in a group over on the right side of the class in front of the cloakroom, facing the window, and recited together with much expression, now loud, now soft, now fast, now slow, the rhythmic stanzas that told the story of a boy whose mother wandered downtown and never came back. I never felt so much a part of the class as in those moments; for a little while, in the sound of our voices blended together—they sounded weightier and more adult in unison—I lost the sense of isolation I usually felt at school. When we whispered the final stanza that

27

begins "J. J. M. M. W. G. Du P.," a chill went down my back as our words came slower, our voices trailing off in the end to a wispy nothing: "you-must-never-go-down-to-the-end-of-the-town-if-you-*don't-go-down*-with-*me*."

Sometimes Mrs. Higgins would put a high-backed wooden armchair in the front of the room, and one by one each student would get to sit in the chair and tell a story. The best storyteller—and my favorite girl in the class—was Roberta Schwartz. Her mother was Catholic, and her father was Jewish. Roberta had tightly curled dark brown hair, which she wore long and off the forehead, clear rosy skin, and shiny dark eyes. Her voice, which went with her rosy, soft complexion, was liquid and full of promise.

Roberta told a story about a princess who lived in a castle under the sea. As the princess moved from room to room, you could see the light of her lamp as it shone through the castle windows and out through the darkened waters. The princess was threatened by an alligator who moved around on the sandy ocean floor outside the castle. I can still see the gleam of that mysterious light, imagine the frail beauty of the princess as she moved from room to room, and hear the promise in Roberta's voice, which told us with every syllable that she had nothing but good things in store. As long as she was up there telling her story, I was safe in the enchantment. And we were all together somehow, protected from the vicissitudes of life and school by her spell.

One day Mrs. Higgins invited us to tell her what we wanted to be when we grew up. One by one we left our seats, approached Mrs. Higgins's desk, where she put her arm around us, and we whispered our dreams in her ear. Mine was to be a bareback rider in the circus. A ballerina in pink tulle and sequined top floating gracefully above the back of a dapple grey horse with plumes on its head. The ballerina flips backward landing firmly in her dainty slippers on the horse's rump, ethereal yet real, her legs and feet delicious in pale tights while everyone oohs and aahs. The horse canters, the music plays, the turf gives off its aroma, the lights their heat, and the adoring crowd gazes at the beauty of this being. These were things worth aiming for. I don't know what the other girls said they wanted—I thought I heard one or two whisper "mother" into Mrs. Higgins's waiting ear—but I knew that being a bareback rider was for me.

I knew, too, from a certain blankness in her reaction that my choice was not what was expected. I had failed this little test that wasn't a test. Just like the time we got to order a book from a list the school provided, and I picked *A Treasury of Laughs*. From the look on the face of the teacher who took the orders I knew that my choice wasn't the right one. But it was the only book I could see enjoying. And did I ever get my money's worth! I learned a large number of the jokes by heart and would bombard visitors to my parents' apartment with them:

> There was a young lady from Lynn,
> Who was so excessively thin,
> That when she essayed
> To drink lemonade
> She slipped through the straw and fell in!

It surprises me now that I ever made such choices. For most of my life, I've thought of myself as a serious, brainy person, identified with books and scholastic achievements. *A Treasury of Laughs*? Bareback rider in the circus? Who was that? Like most adults, I've never taken seriously children's notions about what they want to be when they grow up—fireman, policeman—and assumed that my yearning to be a bareback rider had been totally unrealistic. Now I'm not so sure.

Long after I'd forgotten about such things, I was travelling out west with my husband. We spent a night and a morning in Yellowstone Park, and the whole time we were there I was beside myself with happiness; it seemed the most wonderful place in the world. After I got home, it came back to me that when Mrs. Higgins asked us in third grade where in the world we most wanted to go, Yellowstone Park had been my answer.

———

But storytelling and visions of the future had little to do with the daily business of Mrs. Higgins's class, which reminded me of breakfast cereal without milk or sugar. Though I.G. Op. 3 (our official name) stood for Intellectually Gifted Opportunity class, we were not challenged or stimulated; it was sameness and regularity that characterized our days, especially that feature of them known as the "log." The log was an account of our activities written by each student at the end of the school day. Though the days were very similar to one another, and though we had all done the same things on any given day, nevertheless, each day a number of students would be asked to come up to the front of the room and read from their logs.

The classic opening line of a log was "When we came in this morning we hung up our coats and sat down." Most commonly the next line was "Then we did arithmetic." Or "Then we *had* arithmetic." No details about arithmetic, or whatever it was we did, were supplied. The next line would then begin: "When we were finished," or, as Erica Kramer always said, "When we were through with that" (with the slight implication of good riddance, I always thought), and so on to the next activity—in a long list stretching to the end of the day. The only variations were in verbal style and manner of delivery.

We became attuned to differences in diction and word order (my "were finished"; Erica's "were through with that") since they were the only things to listen for, and we became sensitive to pronunciation, intonation, pace, the timbre of a voice, and the way a person held his or her notebook. Erica Kramer was businesslike, matter-of-fact, with her flat voice, definite pronunciation, consonants sharp and clear. Joanne Jones was comforting; she read her log like a bedtime story, smiling, holding her notebook carefully, smoothing the pages with her hand, pleased with herself. Roberta Schwartz was dramatic, emotional, her log imbued with her spirit of adventure straining against the sameness of events. Daniel Solomon's log was fun, his deep good humor coming through somehow despite the drab recital, as he spit his way through the words he'd written (Daniel Solomon couldn't speak without spraying the air). As each person read, you could feel his or her individual qualities, like flavors, tincturing the dry mix of daily business. The reading of logs was boring, but it was comforting: partly on account of this personal quality that came through, because all the logs were the same, and partly because you didn't have to worry about what you'd get wrong reading a log. It wasn't a test.

One day, across the dry routine of reading logs, a comet flashed. We were going to see a movie. A *movie!* In 1948, before practically anybody had television, movies were a big thing for kids. Such a fuss had been made about it beforehand. When the day arrived, there were the inevitable standings on line, and then at long last we filed down the corridor, up the stairs, around the corner, into our seats. Complete silence. The usual routine.

The film came on. It was about hygiene. In black-and-white—really several shades of gray—the images all fuzzy and jumping slightly. Scene jerked into scene, going abruptly from one long, monotonous shot to another. In one scene that was supposed to be about washing your hands (as if we didn't already know about that by the third grade) a boy with his back turned to us was doing something—we couldn't see what—at a sink. He did it for a long time. I kept thinking something had gone wrong, that there had been some mistake. This couldn't be what the teachers had been talking about for weeks. There had to be more to the movie than this. But there wasn't.

That's childhood, I hear the old commanding voice inside me say. *Growing up is a process of having your expectations dashed and learning that it isn't the end of the world. You expected too much of school and probably still do. No wonder you were disappointed.*

And yet I can't help believing that there must have been a better way. If I hadn't been so scared of school, I might have been angry. If I could have let myself, I would have been livid with rage at what was imposed on us at P.S. 98. I felt my mind was being flattened between the iron panels of an enormous pressing mechanism whose goal was to produce something absolutely flat as to shape, and as to color, a characterless beige. I never understood why it was necessary to be subjected day after day to a boredom so complete it was a form of torture. My friend Marianna tells me that her children come home from school happy and excited, that they don't like days off, and I think of how wonderful that must be.

But recently I learned that my experience may still be the norm. "Hundreds of thousands of bright American students sit bored in classes where the teacher rehashes lessons they already know," runs the opening sentence in a front-page story from the *Washington Post*, based on a study just released by the Department of Education. My strong suspicion is that the so-called gifted students aren't the only ones who are bored. At P.S. 98 it was the structure of learning that was so stultifying, the repetitiousness, the formulaic quality. Under that regime, the students who couldn't read, as well as the average readers, had to have been just as bored as those who read too well. For I doubt if it really is a question, as the *Washington Post* article says, of schools neglecting the brightest students. It is the way all students are taught that makes school boring.

The pain of school for me was such that when I recall walking down Seaman Avenue in the morning, I can still feel it in my stomach. I never was able to express in any other way the anger and disappointment that filled me. In trying to understand my reactions to school, especially the intensity of my fear, I realized that my feelings must have been shaped in part by the person I was before I went there. So I took myself back in memory to that other school we call home, to see what I could see.

3

FOYER

When I go home, in my mind, the place that draws me back is the foyer, the long wide hall that ran the length of my family's apartment. I go there and stand in the dark outside my parents' room. It's afternoon, I've just come home from school, and my mother is taking a nap. I stand in the space outside the door, in the darkest part of the foyer, and do nothing. I wait. There's tightness in my throat, the feeling of wanting to cry. Emptiness creeps in from the corners of the apartment, rises from the floors, comes out of the walls. If I go to my room, it will be light there, but the emptiness will be worse. I will stand in the foyer, sit on the floor when I get tired, not give up. I will wait.

If I approach the door, turn the glass knob, peer into the semi-twilight, go over to my mother lying on the bed, I will have disturbed her. I'll know, after I'm in the room, that I've made a mistake. But sometimes I'd interrupt her anyway, and after her faint moans of exasperation, I think my mother would promise me that she'd get up in a little while, and we'd do this or that, and then I could go to my room in the expectation of something.

Mostly, though, I didn't disturb her, and that is why I need to stand there and let the loneliness sink in. Whenever I go there, in my mind, I

34

feel the same way, empty and deprived. This is not a cave on a desert island, not a dungeon in a palace by the sea. It is not the poorhouse or the scullery of a mean maiden aunt or a foster mother's closet. I am not Oliver Twist or Harriet Jacobs. My mother hardly ever raised a hand to me. She is only sleeping, or trying to sleep. I am safe, warm, well-dressed. The apartment is clean, attractive.

Nevertheless, I imagine a scenario in which I stay there until I'm tired and lie down on the floor and go to sleep. My mother finishes her nap, gets up, opens the door, and finds me lying there, a pitiful heap. Her heart is softened—she'll nap no more.

But then, I ask, why should my mother be my only playmate? Isn't there something wrong? Shouldn't I be going over to other children's houses? The other kids in my class lived far away. None were in the neighborhood. I was too small to be out on my own. In my building were only the Hayes kids and Maria Aherne. Have they come home from Good Shepherd yet? Do I go upstairs to find out? I was very shy as a little girl and hesitant to reach out. It is quiet in the apartment, though the occasional sounds of ongoing life are heard. The noise of people getting off the elevator, car wheels rumbling on the street. Steam noise from the radiators, clanging, a creak from the wooden floor. A soft sound from my mother pursuing her sleep. Then everything is quiet. The noises hurt because they signal that other people are leading their lives in contentment; while I stand here, my sorrow turning to frustration.

Recalling this scene, I've been able to understand what happens to me when waiting for someone who arrives late at a restaurant or an airport. A few minutes' unexpected loneliness and I am wiped out. I'll be in a perfectly good mood, sitting in a restaurant waiting for my husband to arrive, pleased to be there, looking around me and enjoying the scene. This lasts for five minutes, maximum. After that, no matter what, if he's late, nothing can stop the existential drain. The corners of my mouth turn down, and I acquire the look of a displaced person. This happens while beautifully dressed people chatter to each other and waiters rush by.

As I sit there I think, life is for other people—the people in the restaurant, the waiters, the cooks, everybody but me. When I was little, life was for other children, the ones in my class or my friends, Mary Ellen and Betty Ann Hayes. That was the classic standing-in-the-foyer situation: life is for them, and this feeling of emptiness is for me.

The emptiness and loneliness became for me a touchstone; they betokened (I thought) a truth about myself: that I was not loveable, that I was both *too much* and wanting in some mysterious unnamed thing. The feelings had no basis in reality. My mother was devoted to me; she wanted only the best for me in every way and did everything in her power to make sure I had all I could possibly need for my happiness and security. But as for me, I didn't know that her naps didn't mean she didn't love me; I extrapolated my own truth from them.

Sylvia Ashton-Warner, in *Teacher*, tells about a European boy named Dennis who was in her class in the Maori school where she taught. Dennis, she says, was

> the victim of a respectable, money-making, well-dressed mother who thrashes him, and at five he has already had his first nervous breakdown. "I'm not frightened of anything!" he cries.
>
> "Is Dennis afraid of anything?" I asked his young pretty mother in her big car.
>
> "Dennis? He won't even let the chickens come near him."
>
> "Did you have a dream?" I asked Dennis after his afternoon rest.
>
> "Yes I did."
>
> "Well then . . . where's some chalk and a blackboard?"
>
> Later when I walked that way there was a dreadful brown ghost with purple eyes facing a red alligator on a roadway. I know I have failed with Dennis. I've never had his fear words. His mother had defeated me. During the morning output period—when everyone else is painting, claying, dancing, quarrelling, singing, drawing, talking, writing or building—Dennis is picking up my things from

the floor and straightening the mats, and the picture I have of his life waiting for him, another neurotic, pursued by the fear unnameable, is not one of comfort.

This story rings a bell. It's not that my mother thrashed me, or made money, or had a big car. Far from it. My mother had a master's degree in creative education from NYU. She was concerned about the same things Sylvia Ashton-Warner writes about, the same things that concern me! Still, I identify with Dennis, afraid of everything, picking up the teacher's things and straightening the mats. Doing whatever I could to get the teacher's praise, so desperate for it and afraid of offending that these needs ruled my behavior completely. When Ashton-Warner describes the other children "dancing, singing, quarrelling, claying"—I know I am not among them, not because I couldn't dance or sing, but because of the element of joyous, raucous freedom her words imply. Pursued by the fear unnameable, I wet my bed and got 100 on my tests. The tumultuous inside of the P.S. 98 school bus—like the volcanic energy of the Maori children—I never thought of as having any part in me.

Now, after many years of feeling that my mother was obscurely to blame for my feelings of inadequacy and isolation, I've come to see her differently. I see not only the strengths I always knew were there—her intelligence, her spunk, her physical attractiveness, her love of fun, her loyalty—but also, behind and through them all, her fierce, tenacious love. While I was growing up, I used to wish that she was like the mothers I saw in magazine ads and the illustrations of children's stories: a mother who wore an apron, baked pies, and murmured reassuring words as she clasped me to her large, soft breast. Instead my mother was, and is, athletic, intellectual, outspoken, and fond of making fun of sentiment and frills. She was and continues to be extremely tough. This toughness was a strength I drew on without knowing it; I have had throughout my whole life someone standing behind me who was not easily intimidated, who would not give up without a fight, and who was there for me in a

37

pinch, whether I wanted her to be or not. I bathed all unawares in the strong, unswerving, never-stopping current of my mother's love.

And why was your mother asleep when you came home from school? says the kind voice, patiently.

Well, she suffered from insomnia. In the mornings, she'd sleep while my father and I had breakfast because she needed to sleep when she could. In the afternoons, she took a regularly scheduled nap, to help her rest if she hadn't had any sleep the night before. It wasn't that she was always napping when I came home from school—at lunchtime she wasn't—but in the afternoons that's how I remember it, mainly. My guess is that she was coping with her own problems through relaxation, for she was recovering, I think, from her own childhood.

———

My mother had been sent to the Convent of the Sacred Heart in Sag Harbor, Long Island, to receive her schooling from the age of about eight or nine until she graduated from twelfth grade. No wonder she was interested in creative education! As a result of that school's neanderthal educational practices, cloistered social environment, and destructive psychological atmosphere, she dropped out of Hunter College after her first year, unable to cope in a world the convent hadn't prepared her for, her career as a doctor put permanently on hold. The convent, as she ruefully explained, had had a closet for a chemistry lab; her graduating class had had six students, and they had received instruction in subjects such as Entering and Leaving a Salon. *Salon* they had learned to pronounce with the French intonation and accentuation: *sa-lohn.*

My mother loved to act out this particular lesson. She would get up, pretend to open a door, glide into the room, smile to the right, smile to the left, glide toward an empty chair, turn, face us, place one foot behind the other, and sink regally down, back straight, not touching the back of the chair. Then she would intensify the simpering smile she always wore to convey her disdain for this ridiculous archaism, and then repeat the whole thing in reverse.

The chief actor in my mother's stories of the convent was Madame Redeemer (my mother pronounced *Ma-dame* with the accent equal on each syllable), as cruel and domineering a character as ever lorded it over the heroine of a fairy tale. In the portrait my mother drew, Madame Redeemer was elegant, haughty, imaginative, power hungry, daring: a splendid creature trapped in the prison of French Catholicism, doomed to play out her life on the paltry stage of a girls school but innately destined for better things. I remember my mother saying that under different circumstances Madame Redeemer could have been the chief executive of a large corporation, or something equally demanding. And this was true of my mother as well. Her intelligence and energy could have taken her far in the business and professional world, had she been encouraged and had circumstances been different. Certainly she would have made an excellent doctor: she had the keen powers of observation, the concentration, the dexterity, the drive. Her father had been a famous diagnostician, and if she'd been a boy, she'd have followed in his footsteps.

One incident involving Madame Redeemer still burns in my mind. Madame Redeemer is going around the room and telling each girl what her besetting sin is. Sometimes in my memory the nun goes up and down the rows, and each girl stands when it is her turn; other times they are all standing in a line, and she goes down it accusing them one by one. Finally, she gets to my mother and, pointing, says: "And you, Lucille Reilly, with your intellectual pride!"

My mother told this story as Exhibit A in relating the horrors of Catholic boarding school, but, of course, the story did more than condemn the system. The tale was a not-so-subtle boast. My mother's intellectual pride and strength, and her spirit of independence, eventually lead her to reject Catholicism outright and for good. She was contemptuous of the Church and didn't pass up opportunities to denigrate it, usually with more stories about boarding school. One of her favorites was about how, at meals, the girls were read to from the lives of the saints. She remembered with particular disgust the story of St. Rose of Lima, who worked as an operating-room nurse. As a special penance, to mortify the flesh, St. Rose would drink containers of fluid waste from the operations. My mother would make a face of utter revulsion, as if to say, can you imagine anything so repulsive?

Harsh and boring as the convent may have been, it wasn't the worst part of my mother's childhood. It was outdone, in my mind at any rate, by her stories of the wicked governess, Emma. Emma was a German refugee, a young woman, and I think not unattractive. I don't know exactly what else Emma did that made her hated and feared by my mother and her siblings, but I know that she beat them. Finally, one day a neighbor saw Emma beat one of the children in the park and reported it to my mother's mother. Emma was fired. But before that was the long period of time when Emma tyrannized over the children. They seem to have been at her mercy, unable to reach past her to their own mother.

Like Madame Redeemer, Emma was a baleful figure, but not simple or entirely unsympathetic in my mother's accounts. Fond of the children, and especially of my mother, she comes across as unhappy, unable to control her temper, struggling to find a footing in a foreign country, and unknown to herself. In the end, having accidentally ingested poison, Emma died.

When my mother was twelve, her mother died, scarring her young life. I think she never got over it entirely. All I know about it is this: She was called home from boarding school and was met at the train station in New York by her older sister, Virginia. When my mother got off the train, Virginia said: "She's dead." That was it. I picture them moving off together into the crowd, not looking at each other and not speaking, under the gray air of the station, noises resounding in its cavernous at-

40

mosphere. It was to the comfortless boarding school that my mother returned after the funeral. She cried every night in bed.

Emma and Madame Redeemer are the strong figures of my mother's childhood, as she relayed it to me. Her own mother is dim: always sympathetic and benevolent, beautiful and elusive, finally fading away into death. Her father, known as "T. F.," founder of hospitals, sitter on boards, is distant as well, but powerful. Authoritative, brusque, active, he makes sudden, abrupt appearances and then is driven off in his chauffeured car to work. In the only scene I can recall in which he has a speaking part, he comes into the nursery when one of the children is sick, and orders him or her to turn over so that their temperature can be taken, saying: "Roll over, Bill." My mother told this story repeatedly with an affect that was strange, part bragging and part chagrin. She loved her father and looked up to him; he was a model for her. But, though she always spoke of him with admiration and fondness, there was a sense that he remained just out of reach.

Authority played a big role in my mother's early life. The governess, the nuns, and her father. There is no one in this lineup who represents warmth and acceptance, no one who stands for love. Only her misty mother, whose outlines are blurred. Blurred by what? Time, idealization, her own inaccessibility perhaps, and my mother's tears.

———

My mother took a lot of naps to make up for lost sleep, and I managed to be sick a great deal. Compared to P.S. 98, illness was nothing; in fact, it was infinitely preferable. No matter how severe my symptoms, I knew I would be safe and cared for. I'd a million times rather have a sore throat and fever than face the tribulations of school. I felt guilty sometimes, staying home, but usually I'd be sick enough so that there was no question about it.

Tonsillitis twice, the second time I had my tonsils out, in the hospital. I can still feel the doctor's smooth fingers on the skin of my forehead, surprised at his use of force, as he pulled my head back down onto the operating table so they could put the cup of ether over my face.

I had a bad case of the measles around the same age. Doctor O'Reilly sat, red-faced and portly, in the dark next to my bed expecting me to drink milk laced with whisky—it sounded grown-up, and I wanted to take it, but the taste was bitter and I was already sick. So many other diseases—German measles, chicken pox, mumps, bronchitis, bronchial pneumonia, the ever-recurring swollen glands. The bronchial pneumonia was the worst. I coughed up evil-looking things in the middle of the night. I sat up in bed and vomited.

I liked being sick. I still do. I liked the feeling of helplessness, lying there, weak, feverish, unable to do anything for myself, in a state of languid semidelirium. It was such a relief. No one expected anything of you. In fact, getting caught *doing* things was the problem. One early spring day when I was recovering from the second bout of bronchial pneumonia, my mother was taking a nap, and I, knowing that I was considered "much better," got up and started to get dressed. I was restless and full of energy. I'd gotten as far as my slip and was standing on a chair looking for clothes in the hall closet when my mother caught me. She was furious. I had no business being out of bed like that. What did I think I was doing?

Being sick was a way to get attention and a way to get protection from the world. My mother brought me meals in bed, and I ate them off a yellow and green bedtray. They tasted good. Milk toast, soft-boiled egg, soup. My father brought me little surprises when he came home from work. "Hocus pocus mineocus!" he'd say, making motions with his hands, and in his open palm there lay a miniature Hershey bar. He played cards with me in the evenings, and other games. I had a safe nest there in the corner of my room, the lamp on the bureau next to my bed lighting up whatever I was doing—reading, coloring, doing cutouts, playing with clay. My mother found a large dark brown board with a curved space in the middle for where your waist was, and on this

42

board I could put my coloring books and crayons and whatever I was playing with.

The world came to me when I was sick; I didn't have to go out to meet it. It came filtered—only friends there—though I had to wait for them a long time, and often yearned for the voices I heard around the corner and down the hall to come to my room; I thought they'd never get there. I loved the special attention people gave me; I basked in it, their kind faces, their gentle, caring tones of voice, their smiles, their interest. It was a warm world; during the long days I could watch the sunlight grow and fade on the walls and on the bedspread of the bed on the other side of the room, I could watch the sky and the light coming in through the room's large windows, and at night I was safe in the circle of my lamp.

Then there was reading in bed. A great pleasure and comfort, for a book made you doubly safe. Safe from the world and safe even from your own thoughts, though I wouldn't have put it that way then. I read Will James's *Smokey* and cried floods of tears. All the horse stories did that to me, but *Smokey* more than the rest. *Black Beauty, The Black Stallion, The Red Stallion, The Dark Horse,* the books about the Godolphin Arabian and Misty and Sea Star of Chincoteague. I think the reason I loved those books is that they gave me a chance to cry for myself without seeming to. I could let myself go, abject, awash in misery, because it was for this poor, abused horse I was crying, the one who got stolen from his kind master and was so cruelly treated, beaten, bruised, ignored, maligned, neglected, far from home, in the hands of a brutal owner. You could cry and cry until one day your rightful master would come and rescue you and everything would be all right.

Books might be sad, but they were the remedy for whatever ailed me. No matter what might be happening, if I could get inside a story, I could live sheltered and absorbed for as long as the book lasted. Books were a home away from home, *and* away from school. A safe refuge.

It was while I was recovering from one of the many illnesses that kept me home from school that I began to read Nancy Drew. The Nancy

Drew books, which took up nearly three feet of shelf space, had been given to us by the family of a baby-sitter I disliked. I'd been put off by the titles, which were scary—things like *The Mystery of the Old Well*, or *The Hidden Staircase*. I wasn't sure I wanted to expose myself to the dangers they might contain. But one day, there was simply nothing else left to read, so I chanced it. Oh, joy. There were over a dozen volumes to go.

Nancy Drew. With your light frocks and your golden hair and your red roadster given to you by your father, the attorney, Judson Drew. And your kind housekeeper always there to make you cocoa when you came home with wet feet. And your pals, the staunch companions, Bess and George. What wouldn't I give to be you! Unafraid you trip downstairs and out the door, energetic, stylish, graceful, full of purpose—in a light frock. Out to find the criminal, rescue the old woman, discover the clue. Nothing could stop you, no trap could hold you, nothing could ever really get you down. You just put your mind to things, and they gave before the force of your persistence and your cheerful refusal to be bested. Lucky you.

After Nancy Drew there was *Penny and Pam, Nurse and Cadet*, and the dark-haired rosy-cheeked Cherry Ames (she was a nurse, too). I identified with her because she was nice and more emotional than Nancy Drew, but I don't remember a single thing she did. She was no match for the girlish sleuth. Nancy Drew, slim, pert, determined, and good-hearted withal, coolly negotiated her way through the perils and difficulties of life, undaunted. A beacon on the path.

———

Though I felt I had little in common with Nancy Drew, I would have liked to be like her. Nancy Drew would not have gotten sick the way I did, and certainly would not have been afraid of school; her clothes would always have been right, and she wouldn't have minded taking tests. That wasn't me, but I enjoyed associating with such a person vicariously.

My actual friends were Mary Ellen and Betty Ann Hayes. Unlike the children at school, they were people I had known a long time and could trust, within limits. They lived in apartment E6 in our building, on the fifth floor, near the elevator. It was an adventure to go up there by myself and knock; after all, there was only one of me, but so many of them: Mr. and Mrs. Hayes, Billy, the slightly loutish older brother; then Mary Ellen, a year older than me; then Betty Ann, a year younger; and somewhere down the scale of years, Din-Din, her broken voice perpetually registering her complaints against the world, which were mainly justified. They all lived in an apartment no bigger than ours. Billy slept in the living room, and all the girls shared a bedroom after Din-Din was old enough to move out of the crib. It was fun there. Something was always going on. Mr. and Mrs. Hayes were kind and friendly and treated me gently; I can see the smile in their eyes. Though sometimes, unaccountably, they threatened their own children with the strap.

Mary Ellen was the troublemaker, the exciting one who thought things up, bossed us around, was pushy and got her way. The skin on her fleshy cheeks was slightly coarse, and her lips were springy—I knew this from a kissing game we dared to play. In her shiny eyes, a deep gray-blue touched with green, mischief was crossed with expectation. Mary Ellen loved life and was going to get everything possible out of it. When we played house, she always got to be mother (the coveted part). Betty Ann and I screamed with delight when she was mean, snapped at us, doled out punishments, heaped us with abuse. It was the same when we played Cinderella: Mary Ellen was the wicked stepmother, and in her ugly bustle and hideous hat she bossed us around so unmercifully and said things so mean that we broke up with laughter and couldn't play our parts.

Betty Ann was the opposite. Sensitive, shy, dreamy. I looked at her once while someone was playing the piano, and the light above the music, as she stood there looking up toward it, showed how beautiful she was—white skin, fine nose, eyes with pale blue irises and black pupils, long shiny brown hair. She looked hopeful, as if gazing toward an ideal. Of course, Betty Ann didn't have Mary Ellen's practical force. She wasn't a bully, and by comparison she seemed a bit weak. The two sisters were like the people from the Ogden Nash poem about the Snodgrasses and the Swozzlers, the people who got pushed around and the people who did the pushing. If I hadn't had my mother and father to choose between, I'd have had Mary Ellen and Betty Ann—the tough, smart, worldly one and the dreamy, soft idealist. I identified with Betty Ann and wished I were Mary Ellen, only without the meanness. But then it wouldn't have been her.

Playing with the Hayes kids when things were going well was the part of being little that I liked. In our games I felt alive and as if I belonged to some ongoing thing, a struggle, but a struggle that had a future in it, where you sometimes lost and you sometimes won.

We dressed up a lot. In one game we pretended to be nuns—Betty Ann and Mary Ellen went to parochial school—and my mother let us have sheets and pillowcases to make habits with. Mary Ellen always looked the most convincing: she managed to pin the pillow case around her face more tightly than Betty Ann and I did; it gave her a pinched expression that made us laugh, and then she'd laugh, too, and her cheeks would strain against the pillowcase. She had a field day imitating the nuns at Good Shepherd, bossing Betty Ann and me around, giving us detention, telling us to shut up, sit down, go stand in the corner, hitting our hands with a ruler.

Sometimes we got into real fights and ganged up on each other, two against one. There was one incident that lasted a long time; it involved bubble gum. During and after World War II, bubble gum was pretty expensive, at least it was for us, and we treasured every piece. First we'd unwrap it, saving the cartoon that came inside the wrapper (which smelled delicious and was worth savoring on its own); then we'd put the rounded pink ball into our mouths, feeling it resist our attempts to chew it. It felt so big and unmalleable at first. But just after you'd gotten it softened, jaws aching from the effort, was the best period in the life of a

Foyer

piece of gum. First it would be a little grainy, and then it would reach its peak—you could chew it without straining; it still had lots of flavor and juiciness and was very elastic, just right for blowing. You'd get the gum behind your front teeth to just the right thickness, then push it through your teeth and lips with your tongue, blow—*whffff*—closing your mouth to seal the bubble, and either take it out to show everybody how big it was, or turn your head from side to side for the same purpose. Before it started to fade too much you'd open your mouth and swallow it back in pop! making that great sound, the little explosion of a piece of gum, and feel the air escape inside your mouth.

The gum was so precious that even after it had lost most of its elasticity and all of its taste you would save it, putting it on the bedpost at night to keep for the next day. One day I noticed a piece I'd saved was missing from the brown metal rim of my bed where I'd left it—it had been the lavender gray color of gum that had hardly anything left in it. Mary Ellen figured Betty Ann was the culprit and accused her; I chimed in. Poor Betty Ann. Both sets of parents got involved. Mary Ellen and I wouldn't give up—I think we felt there were high moral stakes—and finally, a week later, Betty Ann confessed. Caught stealing gum and lying about it afterward—to me her shame seemed terrible.

The Hayes kids were my friends, and though we got in fights, I felt their basic good nature and fundamental liking for me. I was always glad when I heard them at the door asking if I could play; they were my hope of being normal, and I wanted in every way to be like them. Our families came from different socioeconomic backgrounds, so it seemed there were nothing but differences between us. They got Bond bread, and we got Arnold's. They got Gordon's milk, and we got Sheffield's. We used Lux soap, and they used Camay. We used Pepsodent, and they used Colgate.

As kids, we used to argue over the relative merits of these things. Their father smoked Luckies, and mine smoked Chesterfields, and it was war over which cigarette was better. The same with politics. Their Wilkie

47

against my Roosevelt, and later, my Truman against their Dewey. "Wilkie's in the White House, waiting to be elected. Roosevelt's in the garbage can, waiting to be collected." Back and forth. I got tired of defending brands I knew were inferior because my parents used them, and causes I knew weren't the right ones because the Hayeses weren't for them. I just always wanted to be like the Hayeses because there were more of them and because they seemed to belong to something I didn't belong to—the masses of people who made up the world. I knew my clothes were more expensive than theirs, and I knew my parents thought our taste was better. But I didn't want superior taste; I wanted friends. I thought if I could only be like the Hayes kids, I'd be OK.

Most of all, I wanted to be Catholic. I wanted to go to confession, dip my hand in holy water, and make the sign of the cross. I wanted to have to bow my head at the name of Jesus the way the Hayes kids did. I wanted to make my first communion, not just for the white dress and the veil, but for the mysterious something that doing that made you a part of. Because I was an only child with no religion, I felt naked and exposed. I wanted to be in a large family so there would be more of me, more people who thought and acted and dressed and believed as I did, and I wanted to be Catholic, which was almost the same thing. My liberal parents, from different religious backgrounds, thought that I should decide about religion when I reached the age of reason. Nothing doing. Everyone I knew had a religion, and I wanted one too.

Sometimes the Hayeses invited me to family prayers. The whole family knelt in a semicircle at one end of the girls' room in front of a small altar that had a statue of the Virgin Mary in a grotto. The lights were turned out, and only candles shone on us. Though I felt strange, afraid of making a wrong move, the occasion appealed to me. Everyone was on the same level, literally, kneeling on the floor, and that was interesting. Though I didn't understand exactly what was going on, I liked the atmosphere; it gave me a feeling of comfort, a feeling that somewhere things were all right. Once or twice they invited me to recite the Hail

Mary, which I had memorized from hearing it so often. I felt a twinge of guilt because I thought my mother probably wouldn't approve, and that God might not like it because I wasn't Catholic—I knew you had to be baptized—but it pleased me to do this because I felt accepted by the Hayeses and because it was exciting, like crossing a line into forbidden territory dressed as an imposter.

The alternative to being Catholic was being Jewish, like most of the kids at P.S. 98. But being Jewish didn't appeal to me. I visited Hebrew school a couple of times with kids from down the block whose parents were friends of my parents. Nothing serious seemed to be going on there. The children all talked and carried on while the teacher was trying to explain something, and he didn't even mind. Occasionally they would recite a Hebrew prayer, raggedly, in monotone, but they might as well have been reading from the phone book. There was no religious atmosphere that I could recognize; it was more like the school bus.

Besides I knew, somehow, that even if I wanted to I couldn't be Jewish. You had to already be. And I knew that being Catholic was out. My mother had once been Catholic but had turned against the Church, and that was that. There was one more option open, and I took it. One person in my class at school—Joanne Jones—was neither Jewish nor Catholic. She was something in between that I sensed would be all right for me. One Sunday morning I got my father to take me to her church, a kind of in-between place, vaguely in the same category as the church my father had been brought up in—Congregational—but not the same. It was Anglican and a big disappointment, the plainest place I'd ever seen. It must have been the lowest Anglican church that ever existed. With every word, gesture, and look the square-jawed minister seemed to be saying, No extras. I'd wanted a fancy church like the Hayes kids'— incense, holy water, candles—but never mind. I was desperate to be *something*. After a while, I thought, if I kept on going back I could say I was an Episcopalian. I didn't know what that meant, but other people did, and that was enough.

Going to that puritanical place on the lower end of Seaman Avenue wasn't fun, but it paid off. In the middle of fifth grade my parents moved out of Manhattan to the suburban town of Glen Rock, New Jersey. I asked them to drive me across town on Sundays to the Episcopal church. There I made friends with some girls in Sunday school class, and the minister was kind to me. Once a week the warmth I felt there helped me to survive the loneliness of the move.

4

OTHER PEOPLE

Shortly after we moved, some neighborhood kids showed up on my doorstep, curious and eager to see what the new kid was like. When I opened the door I knew I was appearing for the first time on the stage of a new life. One of the kids wore the white canvas belt and diagonal shoulder strap of a safety patrol, dread staircase troll of my childhood. Nervous and at a loss, seeing it, I burst out "Those damn safety patrols!"

That was my social debut—in front of Walter Meyers, Jack Lewis, Bobby Jones, and Patsy Jones. Instead of showing how much I wanted to be liked by the kids in my new neighborhood, I said something completely inappropriate, a comment made up partly of old rage, and partly of a desire to show how worldly I was and how much on the side of those who hated authority.

By the time my parents moved from Manhattan to the suburbs, the days of my childhood terror in school were essentially over. Over in the most obvious ways, at any rate. After leaving P.S. 98, I no longer lived in terror of being publicly humiliated by teachers. The shape of fear had shifted: it was social ostracism that frightened me. Years later, my mother told me that while I was at P.S. 98 I'd been given a social maturity test, and the results showed that at age eight I had the social maturity of

51

a twenty-four-year-old. So much for tests. The truth was, I was socially backward. All the energy I'd spent getting in good with teachers had left me with practically no sense of what it took to be liked by the other children. For a long time, I didn't even know they were important; I experienced them as a kind of static, getting in the way of my relation to whoever happened to be in authority. Not until fifth grade did it dawn on me that, as far as my relations with my fellow students were concerned, being a good girl might not be such a good thing. And then I yearned to be caught doing something naughty. Nothing *too* bad (I had to stay in the good graces of the teacher, after all), but something risqué enough to let the others know I was a regular kid.

One day it happened. This was before we'd moved. I was in the library at P.S. 98, sitting at a round table, talking and giggling with some other students (they were good students, like me, and by then I could giggle in school), when someone in authority, not our teacher, reprimanded us for making noise and sent us to the principal's office. I was exhilarated. For the first time in my life I was being punished as if I was one of the rest. It was too good to be true. I half floated, half bounced down the hall on the balls of my feet. I knew I had nothing to fear because we were the good kids, the ones who got 100s on our tests. As soon as it was known who we were, everything would be cleared up. And it was. We got a sober but brief talking to from the principal (a distant figure named Mr. Rothman), and all was forgiven. But I hoped not forgotten. I wanted everyone to remember that Jane Parry had been sent to the principal's office for talking.

Being caught doing something bad was comparatively easy; it was possible to create a situation that would earn a slight reproof. The part of the equation I couldn't figure out had to do with being popular. By the time I got to junior high school I wanted to be like Penny Daly and Peg McGlashan, the popular girls, always at the center of a group who imitated them and laughed at everything they said. Penny was small and delicate, Peg large-boned and horsey, but they both had an unnameable quality that made me jealous. Their eyes and smiles flashed out from the circle of girls, as if to signal that their power was in full operation, but whenever I came close to see if I could get some, their attention lit on me only momentarily, then flitted away as if my homage was valueless to them.

The trouble was, I didn't really like travelling in a pack, circling around the popular person, waiting to see if her popularity would rub off on me. I didn't like hanging around the jukebox in Kavner's drugstore listening to songs ("How Much Is That Doggie in the Window?"), talking about boys I didn't know and who didn't know me. It was boring and effortful, and I found myself wanting to go home and practice the piano—which normally I regarded as a burden.

I wasn't equipped for this—whatever it was. I could understand studying, reading, or playing the piano, playing basketball or hockey or some indoor game, but the vague fluttering around giggles and secrets—with your clothes, meanwhile, being perfect—I didn't get.

Besides, I resented the idea that getting along socially might mean work. Where people were concerned, I always thought things should come naturally. Friendships were for *after* school, when you could play and do what you wanted; they fell into the category of the spontaneous and unforced. What was the point of being around people if you had to strategize and calculate all the time, pretending things, holding back?

Finally I met some kids from across town who liked to play games and run around outside and get dirty. Indoors, we played duets on the piano, and card games, and games we made up. We joked and laughed a lot— and it didn't matter if your crinolines weren't the stiffest or if your hair had lost its set. It was a relief to be with girls I liked and had something in common with. My feet were on the ground when I was with them, and I felt normal and happy, as if things might be going to be all right.

In another way, though, I didn't value this happiness. These girls— Lizzie King, Holly Pancoast, Corinne Szeglin—were not the most popular girls, the prettiest, the most in demand for dates, or the best dressed.

It was second-class citizenship to be their friend. They were fun, and they liked me, and I liked them. I forgot myself when I was with them. But I thought that in settling for them I had settled for less.

Something about my relationship to these girls, and to other people my age when I was growing up, foreshadowed the fact that I would be a teacher. Perhaps it was simply a matter of where my attention was focussed. As an only child I was always looking up, in a literal sense. Everyone I knew—that is, my parents—existed far above me; they were in control, and I modulated my behavior in relation to them. The give and take of equals, the feeling of being side by side, was something I enjoyed but counted less important than making an appearance on the stage for grown-ups. What they thought was what really mattered. Unconsciously I cast my lot with them.

So in school, naturally, teachers were the prime object of my attention. That was where the power lay, so you had to keep up with what they were doing. Besides, they had knowledge—something I coveted— though like their power they kept it mainly to themselves. Perhaps it was simply because I had focussed on them for so long that I learned to want to be like teachers. To be the one everybody looked at and had to obey, to be standing alone, up in front, performing while other people paid attention was the only thing I knew to aim for. When I attained this status, it took me a long time to realize its emptiness—unless you were already connected to yourself and to your audience by something we never learned about in school.

Still, it was here, in my concentration on teachers, that the love of school took root.

5

TEACHERS

On the day before Thanksgiving vacation in my sophomore year of high school, our teacher, Mr. Bowler, didn't ask us to do any geometry problems or to put our minds on school matters at all. He asked us to think about the meaning of Thanksgiving. No teacher had ever asked us to put aside our daily work before; that in itself was surprising. But more important, no teacher had ever asked us to think about something as if our doing so would make a difference. I felt we were being asked to put aside geometry because there was larger work to be done, and we were the ones to do it.

Mr. Bowler meant business, no doubt about that. He would never ask us to do a fake assignment—like write an essay on "What the American Flag Means to Me," where it was understood you were supposed to gin up something on the spot and pretend you'd believed it all along. Besides, from the sound of his voice I knew when he asked us the question about Thanksgiving that he wanted to go deep, and to take us with him.

I knew this because from the first day of plane geometry when we sat in the classroom with our desks empty, it was clear something real was afoot. No books, no pieces of paper, nothing to be filled in or copied down. The clean slate of our desks reflected the blankness of the black-

55

board and the ready, open condition of our minds. We were being asked simply to think—a request that had never been made of us till then, in such an absolute, unmistakable form.

We sat there, and, step by step, day after day, in response to Mr. Bowler's questions, we derived the proofs of plane geometry. We ourselves, starting with nothing, or with only the one postulate Mr. Bowler would write on the board, created the foundations of the subject matter we were there to study. No printed page clamped its narrow wisdom on our brains. We worked in the pure ether where only logic reigned, and by its strenuous process we were purified and reinvigorated. Much later in life, when I read the first line of Edna St. Vincent Millay's poem "Euclid alone has looked on Beauty bare," I felt I knew exactly what she meant.

Mr. Bowler had a deep voice, though he was not a large-bodied man, and when he spoke its timbre enriched and magnified his thought. His demeanor gave to the work we did a weight that schoolwork had not had before. He took us seriously, and he took plane geometry seriously, and consequently we felt that something hung on our deliberations. The derivation of those proofs, with no external aids or props, became one with my concept of noble action. For the work was elevating. As our minds stretched and played in response to his questions, Mr. Bowler showed us not only that we could do geometry, he showed us our mental strength. When someone answered a question in a way that pushed everything forward a giant step, we all admired the feat, for somehow, in that class, our thinking was a joint effort, and the virtuosity of one reflected the virtuosity of all.

From time to time, as on that Thanksgiving, Mr. Bowler would depart from our usual format and talk to us about something he called "knowledge and understanding." When he said the words, in his deep-timbred voice, I knew that that was what I wanted and that there were untold reaches of mind, beyond plane geometry or the meaning of Thanksgiving, that knowledge and understanding would open to me.

When I ask myself what made Mr. Bowler such a good teacher, I remember something he told us one day. He told us that he had been trained to teach history, but that after he came to Ridgewood High they needed someone to teach geometry, so he had. Not being gifted in math, he'd had to work hard to understand it, so it was easier for him to explain it to others than if he'd understood it instantly himself. His lack of natural talent for the subject was our good fortune. But there was much more to Mr. Bowler's class that made it distinctive. The closest I can come is to say it was something in the air—or something *not* in the air. Mr. Bowler's classroom always felt fresh, as if the windows had been open a long time. There was no staleness or tension, no emotion or expectation emanating from him to sully the atmosphere. We walked in with no balance sheet appended to our names; and just as we produced the proof of the day out of nothing, so we ourselves came into being as if for the first time. This feeling of beginning afresh every day was immensely liberating; it was connected to our sense of creating something.

Now that I know what I know about the emotional fallout of teaching, how hard it is to keep one's spirits up over the long haul, how virtually impossible it is not to let one's feelings affect the conduct of a class, I am tempted to surmise that Mr. Bowler kept his inner life very well in order. When a teacher inhabits a given classroom all day long, day after day and year after year, a considerable portion of his or her personality seeps into the walls, becomes part of the furniture, and flickers in the light. It was cool and fresh in Mr. Bowler's room at ten o'clock in the morning, and the air was mountain clear.

The surprise I felt in Mr. Bowler's course at the pure joy of thinking woke me again when my family moved from the Jersey suburbs to the suburbs of Philadelphia, and I went for my senior year to Lower Merion High School in Ardmore, Pennsylvania, where I was put in a class called Special English.

The move was no joke. Shorn of friends and familiar surroundings, up for evaluation again by everybody—classmates, teachers, neighbors—I had to find my way alone with nothing to go on but hope. The high school was stratified socially in a way that was new to me. On the bottom were the kids in the vocational-technical track who took typing and shop and wore their hair differently from the rest. Then there were the kids with nothing in particular to distinguish them—not looks, or brains, or personality, or ability at sports—who occupied a sort of gray limbo. Then came the popular kids and the school leaders, the football players, cheerleaders, presidents of the major student organizations, and the people who hung around them—well-dressed, attractive, outgoing kids who dated and set the social tone. They were at the top. Finally, a little off to one side, there was the intelligentsia, the people who ran the newspaper, edited the yearbook, got all As, and took Special English. In my other high school, there had been no such group; being a "brain" had meant being isolated and existing on the fringe. But here there was a niche for people like me. It was a godsend.

My mother had made sure when we first visited the school that I would be put in Special English, so I found myself in a class where all the students were not only smart in the conventional way but also cared about learning and wanted knowledge as much as I did. This was a piece of luck I couldn't have hoped for. But there was more. There was the teacher.

It was Margaret Hay, the fact of her, as well as what she did, that made such a difference. The way her fine-boned features cut the air, as if she were on the prow of a ship moving fearlessly into the future. The way her voice, clear and piercing, resonated in our classroom, calling to whatever in us was high and aspiring. The way her words jolted us morally awake, demanding that we rise to the occasion. I had never seen this combination of powerful intellect, moral idealism, and strength of will in a person before. I wanted to win her approval, to come up to her standard, in every way.

For Mrs. Hay we did three hundred pages of outside reading a week, beyond what we did for class. She ordered the *New York Times* for us every day and got us into the habit of reading it. She gave us as the topic of our major paper "Freedom and Responsibility," an assignment whose dimensions I have still not gotten over, anymore than I've gotten over my envy of Carolyn Goldberg, who wrote the perfect opening sentence: "Freedom and responsibility go hand in hand."

In 1956–57 Mrs. Hay had us put our desks in a circle so we could see each other (this never happened again throughout my formal schooling). Maybe because of the circle, maybe because of the energy and excitement of our discussions, maybe for other reasons, I remember the names and faces of most of the students in that class, the content of individual class discussions—should Antigone have been allowed to bury Polynices even though it was against the law?—and exactly how it felt to be there: excited, inspired, important.

When Mrs. Hay fired questions at us in her sharp, lovely voice, we had no choice but to answer. She aroused our moral outrage, dared us to think harder, challenged our comfortable assumptions. In her class we felt our strength individually and as a group because she pulled it out of us. We were like athletes whose feats were mental instead of physical, proud of our ourselves and of each other. A good part of the exhilaration came from our being a collection of the fat and the skinny, the too short and the too tall, the people with thick glasses and thin skins gathered at last in a place where not having the right clothes or the right body didn't matter. It was what you said in discussion that counted, and beyond that, there was the shared sense that if you were in Special English you were special and deserved to be there whether you said anything or not.

I've had many teachers since whose example attracted and inspired me, but none so influential as Mrs. Hay. Small, thin, wiry, and self-contained—her hair was white, but she seemed young—Mrs. Hay had a commanding presence and a decisive manner. She knew her mind and would tell you what she thought frankly and judiciously if you asked her outright, and never with any sense that you had to agree. But once she had delivered an opinion, which was very seldom, we were loath to differ with her, for we respected her so much. On the one occasion when she offered me advice, I took it and went to Bryn Mawr College instead of Bennington. I've sometimes wondered what my life would have been like if I'd followed the artistic side of my nature rather than the intellectual, but it never occurred to me until this moment that Mrs. Hay might not have been right.

———

I had many other teachers whose example attracted and inspired me, or for whom I was simply grateful. Kind, gentle Mr. Reinhard in sixth grade, who was understanding when I wet my pants while giving a book report. Hazel Torrens, who taught world history in junior high. She wore her hair in an upsweep, but fine wisps were always escaping; everything about her was strong and soft. When she talked, we were gripped by her slightly throaty voice and deadpan delivery. In her class we staged a mock trial of Napoleon for treason against the French state.

My ninth-grade homeroom teacher, Miss Edmundson, who taught English and Spanish, and whose big nipples you could see in outline through the thin material of her dress, was good-natured and down-to-earth. She told us a story about making a fool of herself the first time she went to Mexico—she asked her landlord for *sopa*, meaning "soap." When he protested and said he didn't have any at that hour, and she insisted, it finally came out that in Spanish *sopa* means "soup."

In college, Angelina Lograsso and Arthur Colby Sprague. In graduate school John Pope, Marie Borroff, Talbot Donaldson, Tom Greene, Richard Sewall, and Tilly Shaw. It wasn't what they taught or even how they taught it, in a technical sense, that mattered. It was all the intangibles: tones of voice, figures of speech, emotional attitudes, physical stances and gestures. I see Signorina Lograsso seated at the desk in her tiny office where we held a tutorial in my senior year. She fumbles with a button on her navy blue rayon dress and smiles with pleasure at a thought she's had about Dante. Her love bubbled up and spilled over.

60

Every time she said the name "Dante" in a course she taught on *La Divina Commedia* I felt the full force of her lifetime of devotion to the poet's work.

The teachers who made the most difference to me were the ones who loved their subjects and didn't hide it. Dr. Sprague, reenacting scenes from Shakespearean and Jacobean drama, taking now this part, now that, altering his voice ("Moor, she was chaste, she loved thee, cruel Moor"), showed me that you could love something with your body and your heart as well as your mind. When he did the scene from *The Changeling*, getting the timing just right as he switched from Beatrice-Joanna to De Flores—"You are the deed's creature"—I shivered and wanted to hear it again. This kind of teaching inspired me because it reconfirmed my sense that literature really was about life, and it gave me permission to express my unbounded enthusiasm.

6

TALKING IN CLASS

Little by little, in the course of doing what teachers wanted, I became a talker in class. Not the kind of talking you got sent to the principal's office for, naturally, but the kind that comes from a desire to do one's best. This kind of talking came from both fear and love. Maybe the reason I became a teacher was that I loved to talk so much.

The teacher would ask a question; there would be silence. I'd look around. So, to help the teacher out, I'd raise my hand. It became a habit. I always knew the answer, so why not get credit for it? I spoke well and clearly, didn't mumble or swallow my words like other kids; I had a large vocabulary and could display it when I spoke. I didn't do this to be obnoxious, but because it fulfilled my ideal of good behavior: to stand, to speak clearly, to know the right answer, and to phrase it eloquently—what else was there?

Teachers liked me—how could they not?—I was enthusiastic about learning, and when they asked a question, I could always be counted on to save their bacon.

This triumphant slavishness explains why my favorite anecdote about talking in class comes from a lesson in German grammar. A teacher has lectured on *Das Kurslauf des Blutes* (the circulation of the blood). "Why is it," he asked the students, "that when I stand upside down, all the blood rushes to my head, but when I stand on my feet, this doesn't happen?" One of the students raised his hand and said *(meldete sich auf und sagte)*: "Because your feet aren't empty!" *("Weil seine fussen nicht leer sind!")*. I love the insult to the teacher, and the way of saying "raised his hand" in German: *meldete sich auf*. It implies a lot about speaking in class: "to meld yourself out," as if you were playing cards, to expose what you've got in your hand to the world. Talking in class involves a kind of formal exhibition of the self different from what takes place in ordinary conversation. You're putting on a performance in front of a large group of people, and the performance is being judged.

I loved to perform in this way. Doing my turn in front of everybody was exhilarating: I step into the spotlight, I feel the fear, I say my lines, feel hot, at risk, brave, exposed, then bow invisibly to the unheard applause, rescued from oblivion once more. In a funny way, I felt and still feel more at home in such moments than in many others. For in that space of time, borne up by the audience's attention, my existence is guaranteed. I can't not *be*, intensely.

I derived my ideal of good speaking from my mother, an excellent talker, who believed in good elocution and strong delivery. She would help me rehearse before I had to give a speech of any kind at school. I have sat for years listening to her talk, absorbing her opinions, her outlook on life, mesmerized by the drama of things as she saw them, a willing pupil and not-bad imitator of her power to command attention. I only began to see the dark side of this power when, in later years, I would occasionally find myself trapped in the flow of someone's conversation, unable to break in, dragged along by a current I couldn't resist, mute, and unable to call for help. Even more dimly, I began to become aware of my own power to enslave another in the flow of language—always a person subordinate to me, usually a student—driven by need, the need to register my existence on the retina of another human soul.

The terrible need to talk and be listened to and the terrible way people feel when someone imposes this need on them are subjects rarely spoken about in a serious way. The need for attention is huge and sometimes seems insatiable, and the need to be free from such impositions is equally strong and desperate. That feeling of total effacement (and invisibility) when someone else is doing all the talking and you can't think of anything to say would come over me very strongly sometimes when I went home for the holidays at Christmas or Thanksgiving. My parents would invite guests to dinner. During the meal I was responsible for serving and clearing dishes, and getting things from the kitchen. As I sat at the table near the kitchen door, listening to the conversation—my parents would be talking animatedly back and forth, the guests chiming in—suddenly I would feel a twinge, the early warning signal, and wonder what was wrong. Nothing is wrong! Here we are at Christmas/Thanksgiving sitting around drinking wine, eating good food—and I am feeling smaller and smaller, less and less substantial, as if I had a hole in my stomach that was connected to the Great Void. I feel if I don't move or say something soon, I'll just disappear. At such times it was as if something had happened to the very quality of my existence; though I sat there in body, inwardly my continuation in being became precarious. Not to be part of that conversation seemed shameful, an admission of weakness, a sign that perhaps one did not really have the right to exist after all.

I think that from the time I was very little I must have felt overpowered by my parents' conversation, which went on, literally and figuratively, over my head. At any rate, my mother's need to talk and be listened to modelled my own. Talking was being; being was being listened to. I learned to talk and get attention, so I could "be" along with the rest. I learned how to do this from my mother and carried the ability to school, where I performed to the great satisfaction of my teachers.

I love to talk, and so do most professors I know. Talking's the stock in trade of academic life. Sometimes I think I'll die if I don't get to do it.

There are situations that set going in me an electric current that has to discharge itself in words. I sit in meetings, and before I know it, I've spoken, passionately, sure there's some point that *has* to be made, which no one can see but me. If the meeting lasts long enough, I have to speak twice, three times. It's got nothing to do with the topic, or very little; the dynamic is almost physical; if I don't talk I'll explode. The process isn't conscious—if it were, I'd manage to keep quiet—and only in retrospect can I see how I behave. Where two or three are gathered together, there I need to talk, and if I don't, there's a price to pay. When talking is being, and being is being listened to, not talking drains your life away.

But the desperation points to something out of place. I think that in my upbringing, and almost certainly in my mother's, talking must have been a way to substitute for things that have no words. Things like sitting in my Aunt Leta's lap in the corner of her dining room, while she rocked and sang to me a Welsh lullaby, the sense of security and rest, the buoyant feeling of not having to do anything but lie there and be rocked, feeling safe and taken care of: that was the kind of thing you didn't need words for.

Recently a friend of mine returned from Tahiti. One day, she said, she was out snorkeling, and, feeling the buoyancy of the ocean under her, the effortlessness of floating on the surface while gazing at the world beneath, she suddenly started to cry. She just let herself, since no one could see or hear her. That feeling of being completely supported, held in an infinite embrace: so it must be to be able to live without talking. Just floating there, effortlessly borne up, your body rising and falling with the water, only thus could one exist without the need for words.

No wonder, years later, I found it hard to get the hang of nondirective teaching, where you give your power over to the students, and they do the talking; no wonder I found the change irresistible. To perform in order to survive existentially is backbreaking work; to give up the burden of performance, an inexpressible relief.

7

HIGHER EDUCATION

It was in the smokers of Denbigh (pronounced *Den-bee*), my dorm for three years at Bryn Mawr, that college happened for me. It was a foregone conclusion that I would go to college; the only question was where. The choice I made turned out to be a good one; at Bryn Mawr my experience of school took a definite upward turn. Right away, there are two contrasting stories. The more vivid takes place in the front smoker, one of the public reception rooms where we hung out in the daytime between classes, and where at night we drank coffee from demitasse cups and played bridge and smoked. The other story belongs to the quiet smoker at the back of the first-floor corridor where some of us studied and read and wrote papers. The two settings mirrored the division between personal life and work life, though at Bryn Mawr these two aspects of existence seemed less separate and opposed to each other than they ever would again.

My business is with the back smoker, where my work life acquired the shape it would have for a long time to come. But first I want to glance at myself and Jeannie Berkeley, sitting on the banquette of the big bay window in one of the front smokers of Denbigh, to note the softness and intensity of her eyes, brown eyes deeper than any I'd ever looked

66

into, and to hear her throaty voice saying things so frank I was astonished a person *could* say them, as I thirstily waited for more.

Jeannie left after her sophomore year to get married, pulled away by forces whose strength I didn't understand. But not before she told me after dinner in the smoker one night what it was like having sex for the first time. Her voice was lowered, choked with emotion and conspiracy: "It hurts like hell," she said. I sat there with nothing to say, more amazed than ever.

I loved being with Jeannie, whose life, it seemed to me, went down several stories deeper than anyone else's I knew; Jeannie, who was Jewish, *named* things no one else would. She focussed on personal relationships, feelings, her own and other people's. I was hurt and disappointed when she left. She was my link to something, I didn't know what, more alive and real than anything I'd yet been in contact with. When she left I had no other way of making the connection. At least not for a long time.

But the person I'm going to become is not sitting on the sofa with Jeannie. She's in the back smoker, working on a paper on the nineteenth century Shakespearean actor Tommaso Salvini. I'm a senior, I've come back from my junior year in Florence, and I feel comfortable sitting at the table under the fluorescent lights, going through my notecards, smoking, drinking coffee, getting my thoughts in order.

It suits me, this job. I do it well. The research for the paper is largely in Italian, and I like delving into books, especially if few others besides me can read them. It's like bringing back buried treasure; at the same time, I get to prove my proficiency in a foreign language. The writing is satisfying, too. I derive great satisfaction from crafting sentences that have a certain ring to them, a rhythmic rightness—if possible, a dramatic flair. I like to feel my own enthusiasm fill me up as I create a verbal picture. I enjoy the process of moving from the phase where all you've got is a collection of bits of information and few rough ideas to a smoothly polished paper, with introduction, rising action, climax, and denouement. It's hard work, I have to push and strain to do it, but I know that if I keep trying I'll get it done.

Three years before, as a freshman, I had struggled to write a paper that drew not only on Italian but French as well—at the time, I had only a few months of Italian and some high-school French to go on. I'd chosen to write on two Renaissance plays, Corneille's *Sophonisbe* and Trissino's *Sofonisba*, an Italian version of the same story, comparing them to each other in light of Aristotle's unities of time, place, and action, and with reference to Corneille's treatise, *Les Trois Unités*. The paper was for a philosophy course, so, although I didn't know it, I was steering wide of the mark with my literary comparisons, but I forged ahead, overwhelmed by the difficulty of the language, the endlessness of the plays, the brute, unforgiving nature of Aristotle's dicta about tragedy, and the task of coming up with something interesting to say. Three years later, I know Italian, know how to choose a paper topic, know what my professor requires, and know that with some effort I can bring the whole thing off. Besides, it's spring, and the consciousness of sunshine and balmy air, daffodils and green grass out of doors makes the work I do inside my head, surrounded by books and papers, more intense, the cigarettes more delicious.

At Bryn Mawr I enjoyed doing scholarly work, which ranged from the technical (analyzing prosody in sonnets by Gerard Manley Hopkins and Dylan Thomas), to the archaeological (doing research on Tommaso Salvini), to the wildly exciting (finding autobiographical elements in the mystical poetry of Thomas Traherne). When I worked hard, I gained approval from my professors and felt good about myself.

Sometimes the approval came at a price. For one class we were using an anthology with a reddish brown cover, *Seventeenth Century Prose and Poetry*. The introductions to the poets in that volume—Vaughn, Donne, Herbert, Traherne, Crashawe—were the most inspiring pieces of criticism I'd ever read. I remember exactly where I was sitting in the back smoker when I encountered them. They were lyrical and impressionistic, full of passion, brimming with wonder and awe at the dazzling beauty and expressivity of the poems. The writer used words like "diamonds" and "pearls," "fountains" and "sunlight," to describe the poems; I was beside myself with happiness. But when I mentioned my enthusiasm to someone in the class, her sniggering reply warned me that it was dangerous to love this kind of prose. Soon afterward the professor dismissed the introductions as silly and effusive, not real criticism. We should ignore them. But I knew that the person who had written them had put his whole soul into those paragraphs and that it was my soul, too, because his words had expressed exactly what I felt about poetry sometimes. From then on I was careful to temper my own effusiveness. I didn't want to be associated with the names people used to describe those introductions. But the passion and exuberance I felt for literature remained nevertheless, fuelling my efforts.

At Bryn Mawr the work took place in an environment that was ideally suited to me. The campus was green, secluded, and architecturally romantic. At eighteen, its cloistered atmosphere provided just what I wanted: the opportunity to be sequestered from the world for four years in order to read books, to listen to professors who were authorities on their subjects, to learn to write papers, to talk to other students, to take part in activities like singing and acting, to make friends who were similarly motivated, and to date boys from backgrounds like mine. College was a place where I could exercise my curiosity, develop my talents, and test the waters of social experience without worrying about earning a living or meeting the demands of an alien environment. It was a place where what I was good at counted, where I felt challenged but also felt safe.

Dorm life provided the right combination of society and solitude. For an only child, living with seventy-five other people with interests and values similar to mine was heaven. I never had to be alone, could always find someone to talk to, yet there was no pressure to socialize. If you liked, you could hide in your room all day. Moreover I had friends right there every day for closer companionship, and boys from Haverford and

Penn who would take me out on dates. It was a tremendous relief to find I was attractive to them since I hadn't been popular in high school. My sexual ignorance, combined with the desire to please and be polite, got me into some ludicrous situations.

I went out with a boy I met at a mixer in my freshman year, a senior English major who wrote poetry. After a couple of dates he wanted me to go to bed with him, and I, flattered by his attentions but with no desire to comply, tried to keep him interested without giving in. One night we were in his room, sitting on his bed necking. As usual, it started to get too hot for me, so he proposed a bargain. He would turn the lights out and promise to be good if I would hold "it." Well, I agreed, reluctantly. So there we are in the dark, lying down now, my hand wrapped around this *thing*. It was, to my surprise, quite dry, quite big around, and quite long—amazingly so, for at the time the concept of an erection was not within my sphere of knowledge—and, at the same time, holding it turned out to be quite uninteresting except in a limited informational sense, the lights being out. Still, it was more than enough for me.

"What does it feel like?" he said.

Oh, no, please, this is embarrassing enough already, I thought, and croaked out, "What do you mean?"

He persisted, determined to get something out of the situation: "Just describe it. How does it feel?" He wanted adjectives—it was the poet in him, I guess.

I don't remember what I said, but I'm sure it failed to meet his expectations. The evening ended in a stalemate. I don't think we saw each other much after that, but the last night I came to his room he showed me a poem he'd written. He was very proud of it:

> Some love is fire,
> Some love is rust,
> But the cleanest, truest
> Love is lust.

Maybe he's right, I thought, always willing to believe that others knew more than I did, *but* even if he is, it's not for me.

What was right for me, heaven only knew. I wanted to feel sexually attractive, wanted boys to kiss me and make advances, but whenever it got past a certain point, I turned off physically. It bothered me that I was so cold, and it certainly bothered *them*, so I tried to be more responsive, but it rarely worked.

Next to dating, acting was the most exciting extracurricular activity. Probably what attracted me was the chance to feel something intensely in a safe way; you could emote onstage without owning the feelings yourself. There was no embarrassment; there were no consequences. Or maybe it was that acting provided an opportunity to practice feeling, to go through the motions of emotion without actually having any. I struggled both with having too many feelings and with the sense that in some areas where I was supposed to have them, I was completely numb. Whatever else it did, acting gave me the same thrill that I got from talking in class. While I spoke my lines, I was the sole object of attention; I existed vividly in my own and other people's eyes.

It didn't too much matter what the part was—a shepherd in a medieval mystery play, Olivia in *Twelfth Night*—I felt *used* by acting in a way that satisfied me deeply. My body could move, my voice could arc through its entire range, I could feel, I could think, I could respond, use my imagination, be both spontaneous and controlled—and on top of it all I could be noticed, receive applause. Nothing else I'd ever tried did all that for me. But becoming an actress, that was another story.

When people sit around talking about what they would have done if they hadn't become what they became, I used to say that for me acting was the road not taken. But it isn't true. Yes, my mother did say to me one afternoon while I was standing by the back door in the kitchen that in order to succeed in the theater you had to sleep with the director. And yes, though I hadn't slept with anyone yet, the idea did make me afraid, since I knew that "sleeping with" someone other than your hus-

71

band was supposed to be degrading for a nice girl, and I was sure I wouldn't like it. But that wasn't what made the difference.

Acting was too amorphous as an occupation. I never bothered to find out what it would entail. All I knew was that you went to New York and suffered—maybe waited on tables until your break came. There was too much risk involved, too much that had to do with sex, physical attractiveness, heavy emotions, luck, and being dependent on the whims of others. As far as I knew, actresses didn't have an institution to belong to, like a school or a hospital or a church. They just floated somewhere between parts. In that intermission, I feared, one might cease to exist.

Teaching, on the other hand, was familiar. My mother, my Aunt Virginia, my Uncle Jim, my cousin Henry were all teachers. At home and in school, I'd been with teachers all my life. The idea that I'd become a teacher seemed to have formed under its own momentum. It felt right. My teachers at school were the people I admired most, and I looked forward to the prospect of becoming one of them. If I could become a college teacher, I would have gone further in that line than anyone in my family, and perhaps it would be pleasing to my relatives that I was following in their footsteps. Besides, teaching was simply acting in another form, wasn't it? You stood in front of a class and opened your mouth and performed.

Graduate school was the obvious choice. I could go on doing what I was already good at—writing papers, taking exams, talking in class—and there would be set tasks, an orderly progression toward a recognized goal. When I reached the goal, a Ph.D., I'd get a job. There would be no need to sleep with strange men. So in my senior year of college I applied for and won a Woodrow Wilson fellowship, which meant that I could go to any graduate school that admitted me. One bright spring afternoon, seated at a corner table in one of Denbigh's front smokers, Kathe Livezy, Clara McKee, and I decided we would go to Yale. Kathe, like me, had gotten in in English, and Clara had been admitted to the Law School. For some reason, at the time all I could think of was the number of men who'd be there. Miles on miles of men to choose from. Even the name "Yale," with its prestige, and its Ivy League sheen, had a firm masculine ring. And mixed with that was the knowledge that Yale was supposed to have the best English department in the country. We giggled in anticipation. I thought it would be just like Bryn Mawr, only better. Little did I know.

———

The day I got my Ph.D. my parents drove up from Philadelphia to New Haven to attend the ceremony. As a graduation present they gave me a small antique necklace. My father wrote a verse: "How rare, how rare that a mind ascendant / Is presented with an amethyst pendant." I still have the card he wrote it on, and the necklace, too. I was happy my parents had come to my graduation and knew they were proud of me. Kingman Brewster, the president of Yale, spoke. There were thousands getting degrees. When it came time for awarding the doctorates, the new Ph.D.'s stood en masse while some words were said. I was glad to be there because it meant I had come through at last, but I felt strangely dislocated throughout the proceedings, which seemed to have nothing to do with me or my experience as a graduate student.

I'd had occasion to be present at another ceremony during which Ph.D.'s were granted, when I was a sophomore at Bryn Mawr. Betsy Levering and I had been asked to be marshals at graduation, which meant that we walked at the heads of various lines, robed in black, and attended the ceremonies. When it came time for granting the Ph.D.'s, a handful of candidates ascended the stage of Goodhart Hall one by one, and Katherine McBride, the college president, pronounced over each person words I still remember, words that drew me to a life of study and thought. "I hereby welcome you," she said, "to the ancient and venerable company of scholars"; whereupon she placed the velvet doctoral hood over the candidate's head.

There was nothing like that at Yale. At a smaller ceremony in the courtyard of the Hall of Graduate Studies we were handed our degrees individually, but no sense of initiation into an illustrious "company" suffused the event. When it came time to drive back to Middletown, Connecticut, where my husband and I were living (I'd gotten married between my second and third years of graduate school), I drove our car, and he rode with my parents to show them the way. I arrived first. To my surprise, I went straight to the bedroom of our second-floor apartment, lay down on the bed without removing my robe, and burst into tears. I knew why I cried. No one, not one person in the world, knew what that Ph.D. had cost me.

In remembering graduate school, my mind goes straight to the incidents marked by pain and isolation—incidents united to each other by a sense of laborious, desperate striving to achieve barely obtainable goals. As I used to put it then, I could barely keep my nose above water. The work, the difficulty of the work, sucked up all my energy and attention, and I tended to ignore the sources of solace and comfort that were available. Human love and companionship were set at a discount because my fear of not succeeding was so great. The affection of my roommates, Kathe Livezy and Clara McKee, our cooperation and concern for one another; the companionship of other graduate students—the love and friendship of Stephen Feldman, my boyfriend during that awful first year; the gentle, sustaining presence of my cousin, Richard Parry, who had just as hard a time as I did (so did almost everybody, for that matter, though I didn't know it then) all of this I didn't appreciate or rely on as I might have. It was as if the difficulty of the work had thrown me back into P.S. 98, where it was please the teachers or die.

This time, instead of getting stomachaches I got heart palpitations. The doctor at the student health center prescribed a drug called quinidine; he had no idea what was troubling me—and neither did I. At that stage of my life, all I could really see was school and what school demanded. The need to get good grades, to climb a ladder that led to approval, kept me from noticing what else was going on. Precisely because the work was hard, going to Yale had its advantages; it let me put on hold all the things I wasn't ready to deal with yet: sex (I still hadn't "gone all the way"), the looming prospect of marriage, and—I couldn't even imagine it—having children. In 1961, if you were a woman, marriage and children were expected, and I was the kind of person who did what was expected. My plan was to play both ends against the middle: prepare myself for a serious career and keep an eye out for a husband.

I definitely wanted a husband—that went without saying—but I wanted one for reasons that would not have borne examination, had I subjected them to any. I wanted a husband in somewhat the way one wants the right dress to wear to a social occasion. Both Kathe and Clara were getting married and leaving. I wanted the protection of being married, too, the allrightness of it. In the Henry James novella that I wrote my first published article on, one character says to the woman he's seeing: "You help me to pass for a man like another." I wanted to pass for a girl like another. I didn't feel like a woman yet. I was anxious to prove myself in this arena, as I had in others.

But not only that. I wanted to be loved romantically, and I wanted companionship: those desires were real, and my own. So when, in the spring of my second year of graduate school, I fell in love with a handsome young man named Dan Tompkins, who was nice and kind and a graduate student to boot, it seemed too good to be true. I said yes immediately when he proposed. We were both students in the humanities, interested in the same kinds of things (Bach cantatas, New England vacations), were both Episcopalians, came from roughly similar backgrounds (though his family background was more distinguished than mine), and, when we were together, we had a kind of innocent fun. We were young, we were in love, and we knew absolutely nothing about life.

One day, not long after we were married, Danny and I were driving down the Jersey Turnpike and I turned to him and said: "See those station wagons full of children going by us all the time? Well, I don't want to be like that. Making a nest for ourselves and bringing more people into the world, the same thing over and over. What's the point?" I don't remember what he said, but he didn't object.

I didn't know what Danny wanted, but I wanted to do something that would transcend the cycle of "birth, and copulation, and death"—a phrase I had learned from T. S. Eliot. I didn't quite know what it would be, but it would have something to do with literature. The literature I responded to most strongly—religious poetry and the novels of Henry James—stared fixedly away from the domestic kitchen-and-bedroom side of existence and pointed in the direction of some unnamed ascendancy over what I vaguely conceived of as base materiality. It doesn't matter that I now see such an attitude as deluded. Back then I believed in the power of language to create worlds that corresponded to the loftiest human aspirations, and I saw myself partaking in those visions as a member of the select company of people who understood and appreciated them. Going to graduate school and studying literature for me stood in direct opposition to the mode of life represented by the station-wagon people: suburban, conventional, materialistic, without imagination, sensitivity, or appreciation of the finer things in life. Graduate school was going to give me the means to rise above all that and achieve something special.

———

When I talk about graduate school, try as I may, I can't keep the bitterness from creeping into my voice. Though my idealism about literature was partly based on ignorance and snobbery and self-protectiveness, it was real nevertheless. It was an expression of love and the best thing I had to offer. At Yale I spent five years learning how to strangle my love, and I never quite got over it.

In order to shoulder the enormous workload graduate school imposed, I couldn't let myself know a fraction of what was going on inside. It was only years later that I discovered how much I had hated Yale. On my first return trip to New Haven my stomach went into a knot as my foot touched the pavement; during the entire visit I was filled with anger, disappointment, frustration, outrage, and despair, as if the feelings had remained in the air above New Haven, waiting to alight on my head the day I showed up again. I know I refused to entertain them while I was a student. Instead, I spent long hours in the library, stayed up all night writing papers, developed an irregular heartbeat, and on spring break of my first year took the train home to my parents' house and went to bed. I got up only to work on a paper for one of my courses and, at the end of seven days, returned to school. Instead of breaking down or quitting, I did what was expected. I worked hard. I did my absolute best.

In college I had worked out of aspiration and desire. Though I felt the pressure to get good grades, it was a background pressure, something I had internalized long ago. In graduate school the work turned into something else: a contest to see who could make the best impression on the professor, read the largest number of articles on a topic, come up with the most sophisticated reading of a text. An atmosphere of competitiveness, never spoken or named, permeated the classes and the casual conversation. You could taste it in the coffee and smell it in the corridors. Except for my roommates and a few other people, I never really knew the other students; in class they seemed intimidating, and at parties they made snide comments and knowing remarks that confirmed the impression. I think the truth was that we were all more or less equally at sea, but we didn't want to seem so; so people led with their defenses, everyone afraid of everyone else.

The moment that epitomized the atmosphere at Yale took place the first year in a course on the romantic period taught by Cleanth Brooks. Cleanth Brooks was the most famous person there; along with W. K. Wimsatt, Jr., he represented the then dominant school of thought in my field: the New Criticism. I considered it an honor to be in Brooks's class—why, I'd been asked a question about an essay of his while being interviewed for the Woodrow Wilson fellowship I had won in my senior year at Bryn Mawr. But I hadn't been in his course very long before I began wondering why he was teaching romantic poets at all, since it was clear he didn't like them. We'd been reading some difficult poem by Shelley—*Prometheus Unbound*, maybe. I didn't have a clue what was going on. Still hoping that this would be the day when Mr. Brooks explained the reading in a straightforward way, my heart sank when, wearing his little bowtie, his fingers judiciously interlaced, he asked in his mild, curiously affectless Southern voice: "Is this poem utopian . . . or Arcadian?" While I was still scrambling around in my brain trying to remember what "utopian" and "Arcadian" meant, and what the difference was between them, a student I particularly disliked raised her hand. It was Miss L., who never put her hand up all the way, but kept it close to her body around shoulder height, in an effort not to appear overeager, I suppose. In her too-soft voice—another sign of false diffidence—she said, "Well, I think Shelley meant it to be utopian, but it's really Arcadian."

At that moment I hated Miss L. with a pure, distilled hatred—though now I realize she was probably just as frightened as I was. Not only had she shown she was smarter than Shelley (poor bastard, he didn't even know what was going on in his own poem); not only had she implicitly criticized the professor (*he'd* had the simpleminded idea that the poem had to be utopian *or* Arcadian); she had also made the rest of us schmucks (meaning me) look stupid. I hated feeling stupid. Especially since, in this case, it looked as if hell would freeze over before I'd be able to answer a question like that. My enthusiasm for Shelley—what was left of it—had no place to go. Graduate school—I was finally getting the point—was where you were supposed to show the professor and the other students how much you knew and how smart you were; it had nothing to do with loving poetry.

At Yale the fear of not wanting to appear stupid or ill-informed was dominant and set the tone. People were afraid to show who they really were, and most of all they were afraid to show what had drawn them to study literature in the first place. It was love that had brought us there, students and professors alike, but to listen to us talk you would never have known it. The love didn't have a conjugation or a declension; it couldn't be articulated as a theory or contained in a body of information. It wasn't intellectual—that was the shameful thing—though it had an intellectual dimension. Being amorphous, tremulous, pulsing, it was completely vulnerable. So we all hid it as best we could, and quite successfully most of the time.

Now and then, though, even the professors would say something, let a note come into their voices, make a gesture, that gave away the fact that they, too, loved literature. Marie Borroff would say something bright and sparkling about an Old English poem; Tom Greene would let tenderness and wonder inflect his voice as he talked about Tasso or Milton; Talbot Donaldson would make a wry joke about something in *The Miller's Tale*. At those moments, when the human substance of the teacher flashed out, hope would spring up inside me, and I would think maybe I was in the right place after all. I wrote my dissertation with Richard Sewall because he brought more of himself into the classroom than anybody else. When he talked about Melville or Dickinson, he got worked up, indignant, as if something were at stake; his skin would glow, and his voice would drop to a portentous, husky bass.

It was my buried love that kept me going throughout the terrible grind. There was ambition mixed in, and mindless, grim determination to finish what I had started. But by the end these things were so mixed up with one another that there was hardly any difference. The battered and beaten love was welded now to suffering and competition and showmanship, and the capital of knowledge and skill I had acquired, and the huge investment of energy, time, and effort that that had taken.

Not long ago my cousin, Richard, who was in philosophy at Yale while I was in English, remarked that in those days I always seemed to be working. He was right. In the first year, my roommates and I had thought we could live as we did in college. One fall weekend we went hiking in the White Mountains; on another weekend we gave a big party. Clara volunteered for the Brownies, and I took part in a production at the drama school. But after I spent my spring break in bed, I never did anything extracurricular again. Maybe other people went sailing or listened to jazz or worked on political campaigns. All I knew was I couldn't do it. At Yale you were supposed to get through in three years if possible. Hardly anyone did. It took me five.

We complained about the work to one another, how tedious it was to have to memorize the laws of phonetic change for our history of the language course, how many papers we had to write—we were writing them constantly, so many that there was never time to do the reading for our courses. Tacking to and fro on the seas of books and scholarly articles, hoping no one would ever find out how little I'd read, I conceived the notion that I was a fraud, just getting by by the skin of my teeth. It never occurred to me to question the relationship between my enthusiasm for literature and the actualities of becoming a certified professor of English. Later, when I asked a famous colleague of mine who had gone to Yale around the same time I did how he'd felt about graduate school, he began talking about the years he'd spent in Paris, and in other places far away, then paused and said: "We were all miserable, . . . but then that's how we thought it had to be."

I assumed that the professors knew best. They were august presences, not perfect, but full of knowledge and experience, wise seeming, dedicated, steeped in the lore of their subjects. Individually, they meant us no harm, and they seemed to care that we learned things, and seemed to have our best interests at heart. It wasn't their fault we were miserable. But then, whose fault was it? Was it the culture of the institution, which was establishment, male, Protestant, New England—or the conventions of the profession, with its intellectual elitism, its relentless emphasis on being smart?

It's commonly supposed that the suppression of passion makes for intellectual development. When the horses of passion are under control, the thinking goes, reason holds sway and progress can be made. In my experience just the reverse is true. If it's against the code of the group to get excited or show you're committed to something, then discussion is tepid and arguments are short-lived. But when people care about ideas, which means that they have an emotional stake in them, that's when they jump into debates, find the best arguments, hang in there when the going gets rough, and feel the excitement and intimacy of real exchange. For this you have to *have* an idea, as well as permission to fight for it.

At Yale, though there was much else, there was no intellectual debate to speak of, in the sense of ongoing discussion of contested issues. Scholars had vendettas against other scholars—Helge Kökeritz, who taught History of the English Language to 1400, stuttered and grew livid when he spoke the name of "Dobbey"; Talbot Donaldson, the great Chaucerian, warned us against the seductive blandishments of his archrival Robertson. But there were no critical debates that cut across periods and specialties to rouse our spirits. We were all imbued with the doctrines of the New Criticism, which had triumphed some years back over its competitors, so there were no battles to be fought, only a line to toe, though the idea that there *was* a line would not have been acknowledged. At Yale we were too refined to have a position, for that implied a set of abstract beliefs that would automatically impose something on the text that was foreign to it. Besides, a position implied that there was something general and fundamental to dispute, which, according to the reigning assumptions, there certainly was not.

Yale represented a school of literary interpretation that focussed on the formal properties of literature and regarded criticism that dealt mainly in ideas as vulgar, abstract, and nonliterary. Critics who talked about novels and poems as if they were vehicles for ideas lacked the fine sensibility necessary to grasp the ineffable union of form and content that constituted the literary work. Such critics turned literature into something not itself: journalism, history, theology, psychology, biography, political propaganda.

The worst thing you could say about a literary work was that it was propaganda—with all the class-bound prejudices that the term implied. "Propaganda" was for the masses, people who had little education and no taste, who could be easily taken in. The word "Communist" hung ghostlike behind "propaganda," though *any* political program or intent was supposed to be equally foreign to true literature. For literature did not try to persuade anybody of anything; it just was.

And so, to paraphrase a literary work in order to extract its ideas was, literally, heresy. You could talk about narrative structure, irony, or image patterns, diction or tone—anything that had to do with the author's techniques for embodying meaning—but not about meaning all by itself: economic injustice, alienation, the unconscious. Terms like "innocence" and "evil" were all right, since the bias of the New Critics, though they claimed to have none, was Christian and moral. But anything smacking of Marxism, psychoanalysis, Jungian symbols, existentialism, or any other ism then current (unless it was Christian) was strictly off-limits. The only philosophical questions one could ask with impunity were epistemological. How did a given writer's assumptions about the nature of reality organize his perceptions of the world? How were they reflected in his language?

The good side of this approach was that someone like me who enjoyed the sensuous aspects of language could, without reproach, spend time exploring the thousand interconnections between form and meaning (in another ten years that would become passé). The New Critics' retreat into formalism, away from politics and polemics, was perfect for someone who didn't like confrontation, had no politics that she knew of, and wanted only to be allowed to appreciate the beauties of literary language. My dissertation, on Melville's prose style, exemplified a kind of work we did then. A chapter would begin with a long quotation from one of Melville's novels and, through a painstaking analysis of its word choice and sentence structure, would derive the author's worldview at the time he wrote it. I couldn't say "the author" or "Melville"; I had to say "the narrator," because equating the author with anything he wrote was considered naive, an example of "the genetic fallacy," which reduced a literary work to its conditions of origin. Nor could I ever say anything about how the language made me feel (though that was my whole reason for writing on this topic), because that would have been to commit "the affective fallacy," confusing a literary work with its effects.

Still, I enjoyed the tenacious grappling with stretches of language, making the words yield up some meaning other than the ostensible one. It gave me a feeling of power to be able to formulate the intangible messages language is always sending. It was like watching an author's body language: you look not at what the author says but at how he behaves linguistically while he's saying it. The work was detailed and satisfying. I knew it didn't have earth-shaking implications, but by analyzing how Melville's prose style changed, I showed how his consciousness metamorphosed twice, completely, over the course of his career.

I had no awareness of the kind of critic I had become as a result of going to Yale. I was proud of my professors and what they stood for. They never put it in so many words, but if I'd had to say what it was I'd have said literature itself—a responsibility to honor the texts with careful thought and, in certain cases, with information about them that would aid understanding; add to this discriminating intelligence and fine sensibility (not inquiring too closely into what those terms stood for), and you'd have it.

At a cocktail party I attended in New York a few years after I'd gotten my Ph.D., I caught an unflattering glimpse of who I had become. I'd gotten into an argument on some literary matter with B. K. Moran, an

83

early outspoken feminist, and had been dodging her attempts to pin me down, to get me to commit myself (I thought her efforts were a bit nerdy and jejune), when finally, more than a little drunk, but dead on target, she shouted at me in exasperation, "Don't you believe in anything?" For one shocked moment, I saw that she was right. All I knew were little moves, attitudes I'd picked up. I had a veneer of tastes, a collection of preferences and dislikes that identified me as a bird of a certain feather, a person who didn't make certain kinds of mistakes. But that was it. In the sense that she meant, I didn't believe in anything.

It was feminism that changed that.

8

MAKING IT

In 1966, when I got my Ph.D., women's liberation had barely begun; it didn't make inroads in the universities until the early seventies, and by that time, my initiation as a teacher was well under way. I learned to teach the same way I learned about being a woman, through experience. I was not a quick study. Because I was good enough at it, instinctively, to get by, it took years before I awakened to what teaching really was.

Having gotten my graduate education in an institution that encouraged students to believe that its ways were ineffable and superior to all other ways, I entered the classroom armed chiefly with the notion that I must know something, since I'd been to Yale, and that I must be able to teach, since I'd been hired to do so. In the early to mid-sixties, graduate schools didn't train people to teach—most of them still don't, really—the presumption being that you would walk into a classroom and do more or less what had been done to you. At least that's what I guessed the presumption was; the matter never came up.

In the only course where I glimpsed the professor's interest in us as future teachers, Talbot Donaldson's Chaucer seminar, each student delivered an hour-long oral report to the class and conducted a discussion afterward. The idea was to give us practice doing something in front of a class. After my report—a desperate effort to say something interesting about a horrifyingly long poem in Old French about which I understood practically nothing—I was told I would make an extremely good teacher—and not to say "uh" so much. That was the sum total of the instruction I received about teaching during my graduate education.

Though I held a Danforth teaching internship in my third year at Yale, nothing in that experience shed any light on what classroom teaching was about. When I asked the assistant professor I was apprenticed to for advice about the two lectures I was slated to give (I attended all the lectures he gave and graded all the papers), he said, "Stay close to the text." Well, that was Yale's answer to every question about literature, and I knew it already. But as a teaching strategy, it left me groping. Every day the diligent young professor would come into class, list dozens of line numbers on the blackboard, and then proceed to plow through the text (it was a Chaucer class), illustrating his points with reference to those lines. Discussion was at a minimum. I could find no fault with the lectures, which were coherent and tightly argued, but if this was all there was to studying literature, I didn't know what I was doing it for. The young man had been in the marines before coming to Yale, and he said everything in an I'm-giving-you-the-real-low-down tone of voice. It was this tone, and the aura of invincible masculinity that went with it, that carried the day.

The absence of information about teaching was mysterious, but after a while I stopped wondering how or when I was going to learn what to do. By the time I started my first job, I had forgotten or repressed the fact that I didn't know anything about teaching, because no one had ever suggested there was anything *to* know. Besides, in the back of my head there was what my professor had said about my being a good teacher and, right next to it, the knowledge that I was good at talking in class. My mother's emphasis on speaking well and clearly, and her own example, had helped me to be articulate and forceful when I spoke. I felt I was the right kind of person for the job. And the job, I thought privately, was to help students get the same pleasure out of literature that I had.

———

My first days in the classroom at Connecticut College, I couldn't believe my luck. There I was in front of the class, holding forth, gesticulating, writing on the blackboard, walking around, sometimes sitting on a desk, and they, the students in their rows before me, were listening! It gave me a rush of power I could feel in the veins of my arms, a flash of exhilaration. So this was what it was all about! At the same time, I was so anxious about doing it right that I couldn't make the fifty-minute drive from Middletown to New London without having to go to the bathroom. It was all country roads with no place to stop, so there would be an excruciating ten minutes of bouncing up and down in my car at the end, the climax being a dash from the parking lot to the ladies room in the English department building. My nervousness was partly innate, and partly the result of my sense of being onstage when I was teaching. I was "appearing" twice a day, three days a week, for fourteen weeks. Practically all the lines were mine *and*—the hardest part—I had to write them all myself. Who wouldn't be nervous?

My toughest course as a beginning teacher was a survey of English literature from Chaucer to Wallace Stevens. I'd never taken a survey course and had no notion of how to teach one. My training in close reading was some help, but in a survey course you couldn't remain at that level of detail and expect students to stay with you. I needed to know history; I needed biographical information on the authors; I needed overarching ideas to pull the material together—everything that had been forbidden at Yale. The bottom line was I didn't have enough to say. I was always afraid I'd run out of material before the hour was up and have to stand there facing the students, my mouth opening and closing but emitting no sound.

I developed a habit of holding back on my important points, stretching out the lesser ideas and making them last until I could see I'd have enough material to get me through to the end of the period. Sometimes the main points would get lost or squeezed into the last few minutes when the students were already collecting their things, anxious about being late for the next class and no longer paying attention.

About a third of the way through the course, I figured out how to provide an overview of several periods that had an idea behind it—my idea—and I worked hard to make the presentation cogent and forceful. After class, a smart student with an edge in her voice came up and said that she and her friends would like to hear more lectures like that, with the clear implication that there had been too few. I cringed. I wanted to give more lectures like that, but my lack of experience and preparation made it impossible, at least on a regular basis.

This was one of the few painful moments I remember from my first two years of teaching. Challenged by newness and the desire to succeed, I was charged with hope, energy, and excitement. I don't know what I was like as a teacher, and I don't know what happened in my classes— the intensity of being in the spotlight produced a kind of amnesia—but the feeling was like being a horse with the bit in its teeth. I ran and ran, leaping ditches and fences, getting mud splashed, stumbling occasionally, but always regaining my stride, plunging ahead, unconscious of everything except the perilousness of the task and my own expenditure of effort.

I must have been learning something. By the end of the second year, my students sat in a circle. A friend who had her office next to a room where I held one of my classes said she heard the sound of laughter through the wall. The room was sun filled; I was teaching poetry, drama, and fiction to freshmen. An innocent myself, I had put together a sequence of readings called Poems of Seduction that I thought quite daring. On some days at least, the class was lively and eventful, owing largely to the participation of three students.

Bobbi Stewart used to come to class in riding boots; when I ran into her in Philadelphia a few years later, she was going to vet school. She had short curly hair, a dusting of freckles across her nose, and a sweet laconic frankness; in discussions I could count on her to cut to the chase. Diana Diamond had intense brown eyes and long curly blonde hair. In a low, vibrant voice that compelled you to listen, she made complex, sensitive remarks whose end I could never predict from their beginning. I felt honored when she decided to speak. She told me once that her father was a professor, and for years afterward whenever I heard of an academician named Diamond I wondered if it was her father. The liveliest person in the class was a girl named Lynn Sher, whose bouncy ponytail, strong chin, and snapping bright eyes I was always glad to see. Lynn's enthusiasm and intelligence carried the course day after day; she laughed a lot and was always willing to speak when I asked a question. One day a few years ago, I turned on the television and there was Lynn, working as a reporter for ABC. Her hair was different, her expression had changed, but the brightness, the competence, the good nature were still the same.

I didn't always appreciate my students.

There was a girl named Diane in another class, perhaps the most eager student I ever had. Diane had a preppy accent and a preppy look: blonde hair worn conservatively turned under, big teeth, smooth tan skin, rounded features and huge blue green eyes wide open to the world. She beamed at me, talked effervescently in class, came up afterward to ask questions, and poured her energy out unstintingly. I found so much responsiveness embarrassing. If she liked my course that much, how good could she be?

My behavior toward students embarrasses me when I think about it today. I often took students who liked me for granted, and longed for the admiration of those who were indifferent. Sometimes I even resented the ones who liked me if they weren't the smartest in the class, for if they weren't smart, then maybe I wasn't either. And smart was the most important thing to be. I cared for my students, but still and all,

89

unconsciously I made them serve as my reflection. In return for the hard work I put into my classes, I wanted them to love me, to love the material I taught, and to talk about it in a sophisticated way so that I would look good by extension.

Almost all my effort as a teacher went into finding things to say about the texts I'd assigned, since, as far as I knew, good teaching consisted of having brilliant ideas about the subject matter. This was the model I had been given, and it was what I tried to live up to. Year after year I strove to achieve that ideal of brilliance, and year after year I waited for a student to tell me that I had. When it finally did happen, after some fifteen years of teaching, I dismissed the accolade because it came from the wrong person—a middle-aged woman who was taking my course in American literature, the mother of a former student. She told me my lectures were like diamonds, taped every one I delivered, and gave me copies of the tapes; she invited me to a party at her house and offered me the use of her cottage on the Jersey Shore. It was more than I could handle. Though I was going through a divorce at the time and needed it desperately, I didn't know what to do with so much love.

The failure to meet appreciation with gratitude stemmed from the sense that I didn't deserve praise, wasn't really good enough. My other shortcomings came from a simple lack of expertise. When I look back on it now, I'm amazed that my fellow Ph.D.'s and I were let loose in the classroom with virtually no preparation for what we would encounter in a human sense. If nothing else, I wish I had been warned about what an ego-battering enterprise teaching can be. Teaching, by its very nature, exposes the self to myriad forms of criticism and rejection, as well as to emulation and flattery and love. Day after day, teachers are up there, on display; no matter how good they are, it's impossible not to get shot down. If only I'd known, if only someone I respected had talked to me honestly about teaching, I might have been saved from a lot of pain.

In one of those early classes, there was a student who had been laying for me all semester. I was aware of her hostility but had been holding my own; if the material was hard for me, it was even harder for the students, and I had just enough margin to get by. One day when the course was almost over we were doing Wallace Stevens's poem "The Idea of Order at Key West." I loved this poem and I loved Stevens, though I had trouble understanding him. I'd worked out an interpretation that almost accounted for the beautiful last lines of the poem that begin, "Oh! blessed rage for order, pale Ramon." Almost, but not quite. I hoped no one would notice. I offered my reading, which involved two "steps" or "levels," and I thought I was home free, when a hand went up. It was the hostile student, who was smart and knowledgeable about modern poetry. "Don't you think there's a *third* level here?" she asked, in a cool, smirking tone, and went on to demonstrate that I had left out a crucial third step: it was just the piece I'd known was missing but couldn't grasp myself.

Having managed to conceal my ignorance all semester, I had finally been shown up for the struggling novice I was. The student had played her trump card at the final moment, leaving me no time to repair my image. In the competition for who was smartest, I'd lost the last round. That was how I took it, at any rate. No other interpretation was open to me then.

———

The whole time I was teaching at Connecticut College I was also trying to get pregnant. Nothing was happening. Danny and I went to a fertility specialist with a name like a character in a vampire movie; the doctor had about as much sympathy for his patients as Dracula had for his victims. His ministrations had no effect other than to make me feel depressed. One summer day I was sitting with my college roommate on a towel on the lawn of the suburban swim club she belonged to—by that time, I think she'd had her first baby—and she quoted to me the words of her gynecologist: "Grass doesn't grow on a race track." The upshot was I quit my job.

For a year I stayed home, trying to get pregnant. My husband was teaching classics at Wesleyan University and trying to finish his dissertation. I was working on an anthology of criticism I'd been asked to do by a famous Yale professor who was editing a series for Prentice-Hall. After I'd done the research, chosen the articles to reprint, slaved over the introduction—it was a collection of criticism on Henry James's *Turn of the Screw* and other stories—I received a letter saying that the volume would not be published. At about the same time, I tried to get my old job back at Connecticut College and was turned down. I tried to get a teaching job at the university where my husband was teaching. The chair of the department informed me that I had not been selected by telling my husband in the locker room. To this day I have a mental image of my fate being communicated as they sat on a bench together changing their socks. Still not pregnant, I was depressed and not admitting it. "No book, no baby, no job," said a friend, who understood better than I did what was wrong. I wanted to believe that this was a reason to feel bad, but I thought that admitting it would make me seem weak. I couldn't even complain about my situation frankly, much less face it head-on.

At Christmastime that year, while shopping in New York, I walked into Bergdorf Goodman, a store I'd never been in before. Something in the atmosphere of the store made me feel small as soon as I entered. By the time I stepped off the elevator on the fourth floor, I was depressed. As I dismally contemplated the long racks of skirts and jackets, I said to myself: "There must be *something* good about me." And then I remembered: "Oh, yes, I have a Yale Ph.D." I turned around and took the elevator to the main floor, where I pretended to be interested in buying a bracelet I couldn't afford. A Yale Ph.D. didn't carry any weight at Bergdorf's, and, strangely, it carried almost no weight in my life, either.

That spring, tired of waiting for nothing, I got a job at Greater Hartford Community College. On the first day of orientation the following fall, I fell in love with another teacher. It seemed an act of nature, like a blizzard or a thunderstorm, and though I knew what was happening as I felt myself sliding, I let it happen. I had been a good girl all my life, as good as I knew how to be, and now, as the characters in Henry James novels would have said, I wanted to have my experience.

Impelled by desire—I thought of myself as Phèdre—and terrified of doing what I wanted, I used the *I Ching, The Chinese Book of Changes,* to see what would happen if I took the step I was contemplating. "Your pigtail will be tied to the axle of the wheel and your nose will be pressed in the mud," it said. So I went ahead. I left my husband and moved to Hartford. As I drove up I-91 with my suitcases in the trunk, I felt I was *acting* for the first time in my life. It felt pure. Not because what I was doing was good, but because it was completely self-willed. For a while, passion's promise fulfilled itself. But my wonderful lover, who read sixteenth-century sonnets aloud to me, was an alcoholic. He denounced me to the school authorities when I decided to leave him. I had to find another job. And that is how, a year later, I ended up in Philadelphia. It was my mother who, talking to a friend in the parking lot of the school where she taught kindergarten, discovered that they were looking for someone in English at Temple University.

———

Stunned by the consequences of what I had done, I took up residence in Center City, Philadelphia, lonely and shaken, grateful to have been hired as a last-minute fill-in. Conscientious and unconscious at the same time, I plunged ahead, striving to be brilliant in the classroom, not yet cognizant, on many levels, of the human situation I was in.

Aware that I had to work to catch my students' interest, I tried to couch my remarks in terms that would be meaningful to them. But it was hit or miss. I didn't know my students well enough to know what would engage them. At night, in my chair, at my desk, I'd be carried away by the thrill and fever of preparation—Forster, Lawrence, Conrad, James, Mann. I wrote out my remarks in finished sentences and well-rounded paragraphs, working for the apt word, the felicitous rhythm, entranced by the world of language and thought, devoted to the books I was immersed in.

One night in my apartment at Twenty-second and Locust Streets in Philadelphia, I'd been deep in *A Passage to India*, a novel by E. M. Forster that I loved and revered. Suddenly I heard sirens outside; there was a fire at the end of my block, an apartment house, crowds of people on the sidewalk thronging toward the scene. I went downstairs, and in the darkness someone called out "Aziz!" Aziz is the name of one of the novel's main characters; I'd been living inside his head for hours. It was as if the intimate psychological contact with the character had suddenly produced him in the flesh, such was the intensity of my absorption.

By night it was me and the texts; by day it was the students with their Coke cans and school newspapers. The distance between my thoughts and their reality hit me anew each day. I'd get to class, and all of a sudden my midnight prose sounded stylized and precious, and I'd think, I can never bridge this gap! It was eighteen years before I tumbled to the notion that it's necessary to know, on a given day, how the students are feeling, where they are in their thinking, whether they have desires or discontents that aren't being addressed, concerns they need a chance to air. Not realizing this, I was staying up late preparing things to say that sometimes left the students staring and me feeling like a failure simply because we were out of touch.

But things had changed in the country as well as inside myself since I had left Yale. The sixties had happened. The feeling of breaking through old boundaries, the loosening and shattering of conventions, the romance and heroism of protest corresponded distantly to what had been happening in my life. In the early seventies, which were still the sixties in spirit, I xeroxed chapters from *The Greening of America* as they appeared in *The New Yorker* and passed them out to my composition class. I would bring the revolution to my students, put them on the front lines. They seemed interested, sort of. But when I gave them a chance to choose a novel as part of the course material, they chose *Anthem* by Ayn Rand, the diametrical opposite of the sixties idealism I'd been pushing. What did I know! I joined a group funded by the university called the Student Development Program. Anti-institutional and angry, it promoted student self-determination, offering courses that weren't being taught elsewhere on topics such as opera and social justice. My course, called Sex and the Self in Autobiography, studied the way an author's sex determined the conception of a life story, influencing its content, structure, style, tone, everything. It was my first venture into what would later be called gender studies; it felt pioneering—and scary.

Around the same time, I taught an American autobiography course in which the students wrote their autobiographies and read each others' work. The people who signed up for those courses wanted to tell their stories; they wanted someone to know their pain. I wanted the same thing, though I didn't know it then. My own unhappiness found relief as I read about theirs. It was the bond we shared. Through the autobiography courses I came to know my students at a deeper level and felt more connected to them, mitigating the loneliness and isolation of my first years at the huge urban university.

The early seventies were hard years for me. I was going through a divorce and living alone in a large city. I was on my third psychiatrist, having affairs that didn't turn out, fighting to get on the tenure track, struggling to stay afloat emotionally. Summers were the hardest. When the demands of teaching three courses a semester let up, depression took hold. To counteract it, I worked doggedly on articles that didn't get published. Early one June, when the man I had been seeing broke off our relationship without warning, I walked the baking hot streets of Philadelphia, not knowing how I could get through another day.

The despair I wouldn't admit I felt and struggled to keep at bay came partly from a sense of failure in my personal life, and partly from a sense of professional failure. I had come to Temple on a dean's appointment; that meant I wasn't on the tenure track and *that* meant, though I didn't know it at the time, that in the university hierarchy I was a person of no account. No one in my department seemed to know who I was or even to notice that I existed. After a while I began to feel as if I wore an invisible cloak, so deep was the anonymity that surrounded me.

What could the matter be? I knew that professionally speaking I had the right credentials and that people who counted had thought well of me. At Yale, as I was about to start my dissertation, they'd offered me a teaching job—I was one of two graduate students chosen. I didn't take it because of heart palpitations—my body speaking to me in a language I didn't understand. I turned it down and finished my dissertation instead. So at Temple I sometimes felt like a princess in disguise, waiting until someone discovered who I really was. When no one did, I began to suspect that something had gone terribly wrong, but I was at a loss to know what it might be. I had, to put it mildly, no political sense.

For much longer than practically anyone else I knew, male or female, I continued to believe that if I worked hard and did my best, I would be rewarded. When I first began to teach, it never occurred to me to find out who the powerful people in my department were, or to figure out how to impress them. I thought that professional advancement was the same as getting good grades in school: you did your best, and people would notice and give you a gold star.

Nor did it occur to me that anything other than merit would contribute to my advancement. I was unaware that coming from a white middle-class family of Northern European origin, having what were considered good manners and a cultured accent, having parents who read a lot, listened to classical music, went to the theater, and included writers and artists among their friends, had anything to do with my success thus far. Not knowing that these things had been working for me, I had no idea what could be working against me. Until the day I walked into the chairman's office at Temple and asked to be put on the tenure track.

I was sure I was qualified, since my degree was from Yale and I already had two or three publications, whereas the two young men in my field who *were* on the tenure track didn't have their degrees yet and hadn't published a thing. The chairman looked down at me with his kind blue eyes and explained. The department couldn't put me on the tenure track because the young men in question were "men with families." "Certain commitments had been made," and, since their credentials weren't as good as mine, if we all came up for tenure together I would get it and they wouldn't. And that wouldn't be fair.

I looked up into his blue eyes and nodded my head. I understood his logic; it *wouldn't* be fair. Still nodding, I turned and left the office, but even as I walked out, I sensed that some indefinable thing was wrong. What was it? I had a Yale Ph.D.; I had publications; as far as I knew I was an adequate teacher. I had volunteered for service activities in the department; I was presentable looking. I had no criminal record. So why didn't they want me? Well, "commitments," "men with families"—I could see the point. It wouldn't be fair.

But where did that leave me? I needed a job. I had done everything right. And yet they preferred people who hadn't done as well, at least not yet. Was there something wrong with me I didn't know about? something even my best friends wouldn't tell me?

I went around repeating the story—about my credentials, the young men, how the chairman had said it wouldn't be fair—hoping to get some light on the situation. Finally the husband of a friend, a businessman, said the words that made everything clear: "Do they want their five dollars or do they want the tie?" The gritty commercial metaphor opened my eyes. In purely professional terms the department's decision didn't make sense. Since my qualifications were better, yet they still preferred the young men, they weren't getting full value, unless something else had entered their calculations. With the help of other friends, women who'd been around longer than I had, I pieced the picture together. It seems obvious now, but it wasn't then. The something else was two *young men*, men with families, men to whom commitments had been made, men just like the men who ran the department. I was a woman, an outsider, a last-minute fill-in, who hadn't gone through the regular hiring process. I didn't look or sound like the people they had chosen and had made commitments to—though what the commitments could have been I don't know. Had they promised them tenure? My superior qualifications put me at a disadvantage because *they didn't want me; they wanted the men.*

I was given one more year, because they needed another body in the department, and I needed time to find another job. But over the course of that summer I became a feminist. I went around saying, "Do they want their five dollars, or do they want the tie?" And when school opened in the fall I lobbied members of the appointments committee to vote me onto the tenure track. I had learned my lesson. Woman does not advance by merit alone. The committee voted almost unanimously in my favor. I joined Committee W, the committee on women's issues of the local chapter of the American Association of University Professors. Along with Marthe LaVallee-Williams, Miriam Crawford, and Louise Parry (no relation), I founded and chaired its grievance committee: we scotch-taped inside the doors of toilet stalls in ladies' rooms all over the university tiny little notices announcing our existence that said THIS IS A BEGINNING. We launched a couple of affirmative action cases (they went nowhere). When the university unionized, with the help of other women I represented Committee W on the bargaining team that wrote the first union contract. Soon after it was adopted the university equalized pay for men and women faculty members and academic professionals whose qualifications were equal. The processes of hiring, promotion, and tenure were still biassed against women, but at least the consciousness of people at the university was slowly being raised. Meanwhile I went on teaching literature as though men and women writers, unlike men and women professors, had always been treated equally. It was six more years before I realized that I had been reading, writing about, and teaching a literary canon that had been determined exclusively by, and in the interests of, men.

After five years of teaching at Temple, I got married again. Dan Larkin, whom I met through a friend, taught religion at Haverford College. He was an intellectual with a beautiful intelligence and a deep emotional side to his nature. We talked well and slowly grew dependent on each other for companionship and support. Marrying was probably not the best idea, but it was a way of legitimizing our relationship and of getting that part of our lives in order—or so we thought. Underneath, there was doubt and unease on my part, but I believed that in marrying I was doing the wise thing. I'd married the first time starry-eyed, believing that everything would be perfect. This time, I knew it wouldn't be, and I felt inoculated against disaster by this knowledge. What I didn't know was how deeply discouraged I felt at taking this step. On my wedding night, I cried in the shower. And what eventually followed, followed from that.

The following year I was tenured—the chairman's prediction had come true. I had gotten tenure, and the men I was competing with had not. I should have been happy. I was no longer alone. I had a secure job, lived in an attractively renovated two-story apartment in a townhouse in the Art Museum area of the city. I had published a handful of articles and an anthology of criticism—Prentice-Hall had finally relented. My husband and I spent summers on an island in Maine. Dan and I tried to have children, with no success. I began travelling two hours each way once a month to see a fertility doctor who had helped an acquaintance get pregnant. Still nothing. Frustration and resentment were building inside me. I was not happy, but I was making the best of my life.

I'd begun to feel stagnant professionally. At the meetings of the Modern Language Association, I became aware that things were starting to happen in literary studies. There was women's studies, which I hadn't yet awakened to, and something else, something to do with how people read books, how the meaning gets from the words on the page into the readers' heads. I started reading articles, by people such as Norman

Holland, David Bleich, and Stanley Fish, about the way readers respond to literature. They didn't believe in the Affective Fallacy any more than I did. And I had begun to write an essay of my own on the subject when one of the scholars—Stanley Fish—offered a graduate course at Temple on recent trends in literary theory. I decided to sit in.

It was the most exciting course I ever took. This short, slightly pudgy person, who sometimes looked cross-eyed and occasionally wore something that resembled a leisure suit, would come to class and start snapping at us: had we read this? had we read that? did we know who so-and-so was? And when the answers came back no, no, and maybe, he would berate us for being know-nothing and no-count. He practically told us that we were losers to our faces.

Who was this person? How dare he speak to us like that? I didn't so much care about myself, but the students, how could they take such treatment? Some of them chose not to and dropped the course. Well, no wonder. These were the tactics of a schoolyard bully; I couldn't believe his presumption. But then having reviled us, he started to deliver the goods. He began by filling in the holes in our background, describing the books we hadn't read, explaining the positions we'd never quite absorbed, and then he'd give us an impossible list of things to read by Tuesday. To prove that he was wrong about our being losers, we worked. And slowly, gradually, woke up to what was going on.

It was worse than we'd thought. Everything we ever believed about literature, everything we'd always taken for granted, from the unchanging aesthetic value of great works of art to the meaning of the words on the page, was being dismantled in front of us. Piece by piece, this obnoxious man was destroying the entire basis of our professional lives. We sat there indignant, tongue-tied, at times apoplectic—it couldn't be true, could it, what he was saying? that literature was just a conventional category, that words had no intrinsic meanings, that reality itself was merely a construct, not really "out there," separate from us, as everyone supposed? This must be just some verbal abracadabra, I thought, exercises in obfuscation: insulting ideas propounded in an insulting manner by an insulting man.

I got so angry I would stutter when I spoke in class. I would go in to see this person during his office hours to argue against his outrageous claims. I couldn't get the ideas he was expounding out of my head. I stood in the shower shampooing my hair, thinking up refutations of the repulsive propositions we were supposed to believe. I got together with my friend Barbara Harman, a younger colleague who was auditing the course with me, in order to figure things out. We were pretty smart—we said to ourselves—and if *we* didn't get it, who would?

Things went on this way for several weeks. Then one day I turned a corner in my mind, did a somersault, jiggled the kaleidoscope—I don't know what—but suddenly, I saw. Although I'd lose the picture many times more, after that I never wanted to go back to the old way again. What I'd seen made my hair stand on end. The sheer excitement of it was unlike anything I'd ever experienced; it was intellectual and it was visceral at the same time. This was nothing like Yale, where the stakes had been so low as to be barely visible, and everyone had been so polite. Now we were arguing about the very basis of our profession. What we said really mattered. I think I had been waiting for something like this all my life.

To people who studied literature, this new mode of thought meant that the meanings of words could change depending on their context, which included who happened to be reading them. Nothing was fixed or stable anymore—not we, the readers, not the texts, nor the surrounding world. It was all in flux, all being produced simultaneously by ways of seeing, which were themselves being produced by "us."

Dizzying. But once I got the hang of it, irresistible. Stanley Fish no longer seemed such an ogre. Barbara Harman and I decided we would attend a summer institute in Irvine, California, called the School of

Criticism and Theory, which had just been created to provide a forum for the new ideas. There was a revolution afoot, and we wanted to be in on the ground floor.

In 1977 the School of Criticism and Theory was in its second year. Young faculty and graduate students went there to study with the bright lights of literary theory. The southern California landscape mirrored the decentered universe we were learning to reconnoiter in the texts of Barthes and Derrida. Barbara and I teamed up with another student, moved out of the dorms, and rented a house on Balboa Island: it seemed glamorous and risqué. The faculty that year consisted of Stanley Fish, Edward Said, Barbara Herrnstein Smith, Leonard Meyers, and Murray Krieger, a professor at the University of California at Irvine who had founded the school. I took Edward Said's course on Marxist criticism, attended some of Barbara Smith's classes on literary value, and audited Stanley Fish's post-structuralism course a second time.

The atmosphere was heady. We ate and drank, walked and talked theory. The faculty gave public lectures that showcased their positions; everyone attended; visiting scholars lectured there as well. The air sizzled with contestation: argument, counterargument, challenge, question, response. As before, the readings were long and difficult—Lukács, Gramsci, Benjamin—we just barely kept up with the work. But the intense exposure to a new language and a new set of issues was enough. I went home with an idea for a book, a changed vision of American literature, and the feeling that the ideas I'd absorbed at Irvine were going to change everything.

For me, in a way they did. I'd fallen in love with literary theory. And the most powerful proponent of the new mode of thought, the person who could defend it against the most concerted attacks and emerge with flying colors, who had taught me the basic moves so that I never forgot them, was Stanley Fish. I fell in love with him at the same time.

There began an era of my life so chaotic and tumultuous, I have trouble recalling it in detail—mainly because I have yet to forgive myself for the things I did then. I see Dan Larkin's face, tilted upward toward the light, squinting slightly, serene and abstracted, surrounded by a halo of curly hair. I feel the love I had for him well up, as if nothing had ever happened. What did happen? His brilliant dissertation on Matthew's Gospel was turned down at the last minute by his advisor at the University of Chicago. With tenure now out of the question, he decided to go to law school—an excellent choice, in the event. But I resented having to support him, though I didn't let myself know it at the time; the relationship wasn't working at so many levels that it couldn't stand the strain. What I regret is the cruelty of the way I left.

But I had fallen in love passionately and completely, and after resisting for what seemed like a long time, though it was only eight or nine months, I left my second marriage suddenly and for good—in the middle of Dan's exams at the end of his first year of law school. Can you imagine? It's what I did. I wanted to be happy. I wanted to be true to what I felt was the deepest thing in me. I went to live in Baltimore with Stanley, who had left his wife and an only child.

I've thought a lot about how I might have acted differently. I look back and see my lack of self-knowledge, my lack of compassion, my feelings of deprivation and need, and most of all my inability to know what I was feeling most of the time. But it was not for lack of trying that I remained ignorant. At each crisis in my life I'd seen a psychiatrist for some considerable period, but the therapeutic process was impenetrable to me—or perhaps I to it. Sitting in the psychiatrist's office and talking about myself, I felt no real relief. It was as though there was a lesson I was supposed to be learning but it was up to me to guess what it was. There seemed to be no rules, no tests to pass, yet I felt obscurely that I wasn't passing the nonexistent tests. This was not at all like school, where you could write a good paper and get an A. I didn't realize that this, too, was an education; to me it seemed like an unsatisfactory but obligatory method of coping with difficulties that were getting in the way of the *real* thing: my work responsibilities, getting ahead.

I am not saying that there wasn't wisdom in leaving my marriages. It's not even clear to me that doing it in a more considerate manner would have been better in the end. Each leave-taking had a complex history that isn't part of this one. And these harrowing adventures, in the course of causing a tremendous amount of pain, brought me a great deal of happiness. I married Stanley and we have been together for eighteen years. What I am saying is that my education had pointed me in a certain direction. It pointed me toward books and ideas, toward hard work and achievement. It taught me that these were the most important things. And I believed it. I worked hard all the time, which was what I had learned to do in school, and paid less attention to my emotional life than was good for me. When things went wrong at home, not knowing what else to do, I kept on working hard. I put my schoolwork first, because that was what I knew how to do. And I succeeded at it.

———

In running away with Stanley Fish, I knew I was following my desire for love and happiness, and for intellectual excitement; but I see now that I was also leaping at a chance to enter the literary profession as a player. Through him I met people and found myself in situations that helped me immeasurably in a professional sense. There was a risk involved, that of remaining forever in his shadow, but these possibilities never outlined themselves as such while events were unfolding; I was too much in the thick of things to do more than glimpse the ramifications from the corner of my eye. The "shadow" option was something I lived with daily in Baltimore, so much so that I practically choked on my own professional insignificance. It was hard associating with Stanley's colleagues on the English faculty at Johns Hopkins, an institution that feels itself to be at the center of the universe, while I was commuting two or three times a week to teach at an institution—Temple—that, as far as Johns Hopkins was concerned, was beyond the edge of the known world.

Nevertheless, or perhaps because of my status as a shadowy extra on the scene, my ambition was awakened. The idea I'd conceived for a book at the School of Criticism and Theory flowered. With the help of Robert Crosman, I planned an anthology of the major articles on reader-response criticism so that they would be readily available to scholars. He was unable to contribute when it came time to write the introduction, so I decided to do the volume alone. During my first semester of living in Baltimore, while on sabbatical, I wrote the introduction and a long concluding essay placing the reader-response movement in the context of literary history. The project was accepted for publication by the Johns Hopkins University Press.

Working on that anthology was a way to focus my attention so that I could shut out the waves of emotion that threatened to swamp me in the aftermath of the draconian move I'd made. I sat in the stacks of the Eisenhower Library at Johns Hopkins, drinking coffee from the machine and eating cheese crackers filled with peanut butter, reading my way through the major texts of Western literary criticism from Plato to Wimsatt and Brooks, and the commentary on them. I thought and fought my way through each period's treatment of readers and reading, constructing an argument designed to make a central point: namely that the effect literature was supposed to produce on readers, and what literature itself was taken to be, had changed drastically several times since Plato had banished poets from the Republic. I showed that the New Critics had been wrong; there were no unchanging aesthetic standards to judge literature by because what literature was was always changing, as the deconstructionists said.

Professionally, the anthology put me on the map, so that I at least existed. Experientially, it gave me the confidence to strike out on my own the next time. Writing was a gut-wrenching proposition, full of self-doubt, painful revisions, and last-ditch efforts. But having done one thing that succeeded gave me the courage to go on, if not the expectation of success.

———

I believed in the theoretical ideas that motivated the anthology of criticism; they were not unconnected to my life. They had come to me through Stanley Fish and had to some degree been responsible for our relationship. But they weren't my ideas. At Irvine another student had given me a T-shirt as a good-bye present. She'd had it specially made. On it were the words "Organic Intellectual," a phrase from Gramsci that referred to someone whose philosophy had sprung directly from the circumstances of her life. I was honored by this designation, for it put into words exactly the kind of person I wanted to become. And in a way, it did happen.

I had come home from the School of Criticism and Theory, charged with the determination to educate myself in the context of American literature. For my entire life as a student I had been told to pay attention only to the "text itself"; focussing on anything else—the author's life, the historical events that took place during the period when the work was written—was strictly off-limits, a vulgar and inadequate substitute for communion with the work itself. But now I was armed with the conviction that one could not understand literature in isolation from its conditions of production, so I audited a course in the history of American popular culture and read *Uncle Tom's Cabin* for the first time.

When I read that book and felt its amazing power, I knew something had been wrong with my literary education, something not accidental or superficial but systematic and deep. This was unquestionably one of the greatest books I had ever read. It was inspired, eloquent, dazzling. I cried more than once when I read it—something I almost never did in those days, either when reading or in any other situation. But not once in all my years of schooling had anyone ever suggested that this book was worth reading; on the contrary, when Stowe's novel was mentioned, which was seldom, it was in a dismissive or condescending way.

Then and there I decided to fight for that book. To fight for my tears, and for the legitimacy of my reactions to literature all across the board. No matter what anyone said about propaganda or the affective fallacy or the sentimentality of women's writing, I would refuse to buy into any critical position that did not admit the importance of such work. It was a liberating moment. From then on my energy was focussed in a way it had never been before. At last I was fighting for myself, by fighting for a book that had moved me to the core.

It was exhilarating to be able to throw my weight behind a position that had something to do with my own life and with the women writers I felt were my allies, living and dead. I wanted to set the record straight where women and literature were concerned. I wanted to make sure people knew it wasn't true what students of American literature had been taught all along, namely, that all the great classics of the nineteenth century had been written by men, and (with the exception of Emily Dickinson) all the trash had been written by women. I wanted to make sure people knew that women writers had not been given an even break because it wasn't in the interests of those who ran the literary establishment (i.e., men) to do so. If the case for recognizing the importance of women's writing was an only slightly displaced plea for recognizing the importance of women professors like me who thought *they* hadn't had an even break either, so much the better. The same self-interest that had created the literary canon in the image of men would unmake and re-create it; only now the canon would reflect the faces of women and of other groups whose work had never been recognized before. It was high time. Women had been discriminated against for thousands of years, and I was damned if I would connive in their betrayal for one second longer, now that I knew what was going on.

It was this anger—the anger of someone whose intellectual position grew out of her own life—that enabled me to write a book that called for a changed canon of American literature. Its purpose was to expand our notion of what counted as literature to include popular books, novels that interpreted life in a way that moved masses of readers, and especially books written by women, whose work until that time had been used as a foil for expounding the greatness of literary works written by men. I felt that the cultural work of women's popular fiction, its capacity to help people live their lives, was as important to understand as the aesthetic properties of works handpicked by male critics and read only by an educated few.

———

The whole time I was working on the book I felt my life was barrelling down a railroad track. I lived in Baltimore, commuted to my job in Philadelphia, and worked all the time. A conscientious teacher, I carried a full load of courses, worked on my book, exercised, kept up a social life, and wore myself out. When I sat on the sofa in our apartment on North Charles Street one evening and Stanley said something to me that I interpreted as a criticism, I started to cry. It was nothing, really, but I had no resilience. Anything could pierce me to the quick. After the first four or five weeks of the fall semester, I got to feeling that if I didn't take a week off in order to rest, I'd fall apart.

I'd lie in bed at night making lists in my head of the things I needed to take with me the following day. Some semesters I carried the books, Xeroxes, teaching notes, student papers, and odds and ends of material for three different courses. And, if I was staying overnight in Philadelphia, I also had stockings, underwear, medicine, toothbrush, cosmetics, hairbrush, maybe a change of clothes. I couldn't sleep for worrying that I might forget something important—money, tampons, pages to be photocopied for an upcoming assignment.

On the train in the mornings I worked intently, pausing only to look at the three beautiful bodies of water that punctuate the Baltimore to Philadelphia run: two arms of the Chesapeake Bay and a stretch of the

Delaware River. The soft steely blue of those expanses, their spaciousness and calm, contrasted with my anxious concentration—to which they were both a solace and a rebuke.

Though I disliked commuting, I liked the train. It was a friendly place. The seats were comfortable and cozy; it was fun going to the snack car for a coffee and a cheese Danish. Surrounded by books, papers, and bags, I made a nest for myself. The loud rumble of the wheels helped my concentration; the energy of the train fueled mine. I felt busy and safe and part of the ongoing activity of life, though sheltered from it, speeding by trees and farms and towns as I graded papers, or read a text for class, or wrote out my notes. The hard part was the anxiety and fatigue that surrounded me on either end of the ride.

The first couple of years I commuted I'd arrive at Thirtieth Street Station and trudge with my overloaded bookbag and heavy carryall to the subway. I had to change twice—once at City Hall and once at Girard Avenue, before arriving at my stop at Broad and Columbia. Then it was another haul to the soulless concrete tower the university had built to house the humanities. To conserve energy I tried staying overnight sometimes, either at my parents' house in the suburbs or with a friend who lived in Center City, but neither arrangement felt right. One morning when I came down to breakfast my father looked at me and said: "You always seem unhappy." I didn't know what he was talking about. This was my life, wasn't it? What I'd chosen. I wasn't supposed to be unhappy; I was supposed to be successful, and successful people were supposed to enjoy themselves. There was something in his words I didn't want to look at because I was afraid of what I'd find.

I stopped staying overnight soon after that and started taking taxis to and from the station, at least I could do that to help myself. Riding in the dark cave of the taxi with its slightly rotten smell, I'd work to allay my anxiety on the way to school: Did I have everything? Was I well enough prepared for class? Would I have time to do all the things I had to do before catching the train home?

Two dreams I had during this period relayed the tenor of my life. In one, I'm walking down a street in Philadelphia, one of the small streets I always wished I lived on; it was lined with charming-looking townhouses and small trees. I stop at the door of such a house, try the knob, and it opens. I walk into a kitchen, perfectly appointed, neat, immaculate. From the opposite door a maid enters the room. I inquire after the lady of the house, and the maid replies: "Madam is away now." Yes, I thought, and felt a familiar emptiness.

Thinking about the dream I wondered, Who was "madam"? And why was I dreaming about living in Philadelphia when I'd so recently run away to Baltimore? Then I saw. I was madam, and I was in several senses "away now." Not settled anywhere, bombing back and forth between two cities, one my workplace, the other my new home, with no time to properly tend to the demands of either. This much I saw. What I didn't see was my longing to be home to myself.

In the other dream, I'm sitting in my living room with Stanley and one or two friends. The sofas and chairs are large and comfortable, but rather far apart. Then I realize the room has no walls. We're sitting on a platform of the Baltimore railroad station, and in the distance, trains are going by. My peripheral vision picks up dim figures in the background. This humming, cavernous, twilight space is my home. A faint, hopeless weariness comes over me. I'd forgotten that this is where I live.

I had no thoughts about this dream. Its meaning seemed plain. There was nothing I could do about it, or so I felt, so I let it go.

During this time I met a woman on the train who also commuted from Baltimore to Philadelphia. She was an Israeli. She lived in Reisterstown, some miles north of Baltimore, and commuted to Temple University Hospital, which was further out Broad Street than the main campus where I taught. She did this, round-trip, five times a week. The most I ever did was two or three, or occasionally four. I marvelled at Helga. She was so tough. She looked a little dry and wizened, as if the constant passage back and forth had taken the juices from her skin. But for a long time I looked up to her as an Amazon among commuters.

Then one day during spring break I met her by accident at a bakery in an upscale shopping center north of downtown Baltimore. We sat down together and had coffee and a pastry, glad to see one another in this almost holiday atmosphere. "Well," I said, "how's life treating you?" or something of the sort. She answered like a shot: "I don't exist." The words were as harsh in sound as they were in intent, the sibilance of the s, the sharp point of the t. There was no getting around what she had said. She had a husband and a son, she explained; one was a doctor. They led their lives. She "did" for them: washing, cooking, and so forth. I could see how it was. She, a ghost who rode the train and turned up when needed. She was right. She didn't exist.

The encounter subtly changed my stance toward commuting. I no longer admired people who did it a lot, and began to wonder about myself. The words "I don't exist" had a strange resonance for me, ringing in my head long after they were spoken. I wanted not to commute. I wanted to leave Temple, but as long as I was riding the train, I'd never be able to do the work I needed to do to make myself marketable. These, at any rate, were the terms in which I understood my situation. So when Columbia offered Stanley and me visiting one-year appointments, I leapt at the chance. Maybe they'd hire us both, and we could move to New York! Whatever happened, at least for one year I could stay in one place; I'd be off the train.

When we arrived at Columbia, though we were both being looked over for jobs, it was clearly Stanley they wanted and not me. I realized I had to finish my book on American literature so that I could become a viable candidate. I loved the Columbia undergraduates, but I never again wanted to experience the slights and rebuffs meted out to me by various members of Columbia's English department. Anger had helped me start the book, and anger helped me finish it. Over the winter break I got up early every morning to tackle the revisions, waking each day with a line from Burton Raffel's translation of *Beowulf* ringing in my ears: "And then Beowulf was back on his feet and fighting."

Although Columbia didn't make me an offer, that spring the Graduate Center of the City University of New York hired me to teach the following year, with the possibility of a permanent appointment. I loved teaching at CUNY. My students—many of them women coming to graduate school after time off—were hungry to learn about theory and feminism and the new approaches to American literature. The atmosphere at the Graduate Center supported intellectual debate. I loved getting into lunchtime wrangles about epistemology in the cafeteria with members of the philosophy department; American literature faculty from the other colleges in the CUNY system came to the center, and we'd talk about our work.

The department members at CUNY voted to hire me, but the provost turned me down. When I got the news by phone in the room I rented in a West Village apartment, I was crushed. I wanted the job at the Graduate Center badly because I loved the place and because I wanted to be valued for myself, for the work I had done in my own field, not just as part of a couple. And this had been my chance. For by that time, Stanley and I were on the job market together.

The commute back and forth to Temple was too hard for me to want to continue, and after being at Columbia and CUNY, I didn't want to go back. Though Stanley loved Johns Hopkins, he was willing to move. And now that my book was coming out, it was more likely that I would be hired. At the time, Duke was trying to rebuild its literature programs, and when it became known that we were on the market, we were invited to become candidates. This time, there was no looking-over period. Duke made us excellent offers, and we went.

Going to Duke with Stanley brought to an end my struggles to gain professional recognition. My book appeared and made an impression; being at Duke helped. I was invited to lecture, to speak at conferences, to be on panels, to contribute chapters to scholarly volumes, to review candidates for tenure, to read manuscripts for presses, to serve on the editorial boards of journals. It was everything I had longed for in the days when I had commuted from Baltimore to Philadelphia to teach remedial writing and had envied the people I knew at Johns Hopkins with their light course loads and insider status. I enjoyed my success. Having a secure position at a prestigious university that supported me professionally gave me internal freedom. It was a few years before I realized that I no longer needed to worry so much about what other people thought of me—the habit was so ingrained I'm still learning to let go of it. But gradually the truth dawned: I could do what I wanted.

9

ASH WEDNESDAY

From here on, the story doesn't move in a straight line. Like ice breaking up on a river, there's a sudden crack, and dark water shows through in one place, then another, and another. Pretty soon, everything is breaking up.

With literary theory and feminism I discovered that I loved to fight. Girded by righteousness, flourishing my arguments around me like blades, with the prestige of Duke behind me and the knowledge that I had written an influential book, I'd go places to lecture and feel the hostility of the men in the room, and of some of the women, too. During the question-and-answer period I'd make my replies, sure of my logic and sure of the moral superiority of my arguments. I knew I was right. From the mixed vibes I knew I had failed to convince many—who knew how many?—of the rightness of my position. Never mind. I'd learned that holding controversial views was professionally sexy and would get me further than sounding nice.

There's a picture of me as I was then, lecturing to the freshman class at Duke during orientation week. I'm standing in front of a blackboard, one hand on my hip, the other gesturing, making a point. My talk, "From *King Lear* to the Lone Ranger: New Directions in Literary Theory and Practice," was an all-out attack on the sacredness of the literary canon. I gave them post-structuralism in a nutshell, told them that literature belonged to readers not to critics, and that they could read what they loved. The whole time I was lecturing I had a terrible headache. Afterward I went home and went to bed.

Though I didn't see it at the time, my attacks had about them the air of a vendetta. I was getting back at my enemies, killing them with every word that came out of my mouth, and it was satisfying work. On whom was I taking revenge? Was it the man who had refused to give me a car loan after I had separated from my first husband, saying: "There might be a little seed inside of you, and then you'd have to quit your job"? Or the department chair at Temple who, after my promotion was denied, said of the texts I was working on, "After all, they are two lousy novels," and who also told me that my essay on Stowe could have been written by a graduate student?

No. When the object of my anger presented itself to me, as it did from time to time, it was none of these men I thought of, but a poet I'd studied in school. It was T. S. Eliot who bore the burden of my resentment, Eliot whom I identified with everything I hated in poetry, in criticism, in the attitudes of the literary establishment: its sexism, its class snobbery, its intellectual arrogance, its aesthetic fastidiousness, and its bloodlessness. At least, that was how I understood Eliot then.

I had first been introduced to the poetry of T. S. Eliot in twelfth-grade English class. Right from the beginning it made me feel hopeless and despairing. We read a poem called "The Hollow Men," which, by its dry, croaking voice, its impotent gaps and pauses, taught me, and in the end just came out and told me: "This is the way the world ends / Not with a bang but a whimper."

I had thought we were supposed to be engaged in a struggle for the truth; I had thought we were going to be grappling with big things, forcing the protean god of life to yield up his name. But no. According to Eliot, it had all been lost and won long ago. Now the only correct posture was a refined, well-educated despair. I couldn't believe that my wonderful English teacher, Mrs. Hay, so full or moral fervor herself, could endorse such an attitude. But apparently where Eliot was concerned she did.

Eliot's message was repeated the following year in freshman English where we read "The Love Song of J. Alfred Prufrock" and the "Preludes." These poems confirmed what I already suspected: that if I hated the image, if it made me feel stupid, numb, depressed, (those "ragged claws," those "yellow soles of feet," that "patient etherised upon a table"), it must be sophisticated, poetic. If the writing was difficult, dry, emotionally perverse, that made it good, the best. I tried to feel world-weary, hopeless, took a masochistic pleasure in pretending to be blasé. But still every time I read the line "No! I am not Prince Hamlet, nor was meant to be," I inwardly screamed, "You *are* Prince Hamlet. I *am* Prince Hamlet, and was meant to be. I *am* somebody. Things *do* matter. Life *does* mean something."

Alongside Eliot we read Katherine Ann Porter's *Noon Wine*, a story about the drastic consequences of going all out too soon (that was what my teacher said it was about; I didn't get it on my own). If going all out would kill you, I would hold back.

The next year in an upper-level course it was Eliot again, the *Four Quartets*. I tried to believe the famous line where Eliot says that mankind cannot bear very much reality. But I *hungered* for reality, or thought I did, and did not believe what the poet said, although I talked myself into believing it because I thought that that was my job. By then I was down for the count. I'd read *The Waste Land* and "Gerontion" and *Ash-Wednesday* and *The Cocktail Party* and *Murder in the Cathedral* and *Sweeney Agonistes*. I could quote "Because I do not hope to turn again" and the Italian source in Guido Cavalcanti; I memorized lines from the first quartet that I have never to this day understood, and I could think, with a sigh, "Weave, weave the sunlight in your hair," though these lines from "La Figlia che Piange" were suspiciously melodic and full of feeling. I had learned about the malaise of modern life from my professor, Miss Woodworth, who clearly suffered from it herself, and I tried to feel it, too, to no avail.

It was no accident, then, that years later when I finally discovered it was not wrong to stick your chin out and to wear your heart on your sleeve, I embraced exactly the kind of literature Eliot hated: books written by women, books millions of people had loved, books that were full of feeling, books that changed people's minds by capturing their hearts. Every word I wrote on behalf of the sentimental novelists of the nineteenth century was a nail in Eliot's coffin. When I spoke to the freshman class at Duke, there would be no "ragged claws" forced down their throats. If I could help it, there would be no more refined, well-educated despair.

———

The spring after I spoke to the freshmen, I began to get a series of migraines, first one a week, then two a week, that were so bad there were times I didn't want to live. The headaches came in conjunction with an experimental course I was teaching on emotion, a feminist theory course offered at the graduate level to students in the humanities. The course itself was traumatic—that was the headaches' immediate cause; the underlying cause was my life. The headaches were a knock on the door of my life telling me I had to change.

I started doing the things people do when they need to slow down, reassess, get in touch with themselves. I went into therapy, again. I started getting massages. I began to do meditation, took more frequent walks in the woods. My bedside reading came to consist almost entirely of self-help books: Louise Hay, Hugh Prather, Stephen Levine.

It's not possible to describe the way a person changes as the result of such a process. In the beginning, you don't even know what you're doing. I thought I was trying to treat the headaches. I knew my professional orientation was shifting. But these were just symptoms. The real change was taking place in my heart, in my soul, somewhere between me and the trees in the forest where I walked. In the air of the room where I meditated every morning. In the way my dog would lick me when I gave her her breakfast and said, "Thank you, Ribbon," meaning, thank you for existing; I was so glad to have this dog in my life. It also happened inside my head, where I began to watch my thoughts, a result of the kind of meditation I was practicing, which encourages you to be aware of what is passing in your mind.

This nascent awareness of myself, sporadic, minimal, painful, yet persistent, slowly and spasmodically ramified. I began to listen to myself more. At first, this meant doing things as simple as going to the bathroom when I needed to, taking a nap when I was sleepy, getting up and stretching when I sensed it might be a good idea. I began to follow other intuitions that I had—what to wear, when to keep silent in a conversation, when to answer the telephone and when to let it ring. Trusting myself, I discovered, meant giving up control over my decisions. The choice came from me, but not from the part of me that used to decide—the mind that weighed, the mind that projected scenarios, the mind that controlled. Nor did it come from reading my horoscope in the newspaper, but more from the part of me that says, I think I'll have a drink of water now. Trusting myself in small ways—no prophetic wisdom involved—led me on.

One day I cleared off all the surfaces in my study at home, till there was nothing left except a phone and an ornamental letter opener. Everything else—the bills, the brochures, the catalogues, the magazines, the requests for contributions, the letters, the slips of paper with telephone numbers, addresses, lists of things to do on them—went into two shopping bags. Even the cards and posters that had covered the huge bulletin board above my desk came down. I removed the bulletin board and put it in the shed. I sold my desk. When my answering machine stopped working properly, I didn't get it fixed.

It was an emptying out process I was engaged in. I didn't know why. At around the same time I began to look speculatively at my bookshelves, packed tight with the volumes I had acquired over a lifetime. Now they seemed obscurely in the way. In the way of what, I had no idea. Meanwhile, the emptying out had begun to infiltrate my teaching. It wasn't that my ideas had changed. I still held a grudge against T. S. Eliot and championed women writers—especially the most despised. The change was of a different sort. Actually, it had begun a long time before, before I had any notion of what it was or where it would lead. It had started when I was at Columbia, when my mind was on other things.

I was walking down an empty corridor in Hamilton Hall one day on the way to class (I was always a little bit late), having stayed up late the night before preparing, when I thought to myself for the first time: I have to remember to find out what *they* want (meaning the students), what *they* need, now, right at this moment, and not worry about whether what I've prepared is good enough, or ever gets said at all. Whereas for my entire teaching life I had always thought that what I was doing was helping my students to understand the material we were studying—Melville or post-structuralism or whatever it happened to be—as a result of that moment I realized that what I had actually been concerned with was showing the students how smart I was, how knowledgeable I was, and how well prepared I was for class. I had been putting on a performance whose true goal was not to help the students learn, as I had thought, but to perform before them in such a way that they would have a good opinion of me. I realized that my fear of being found wanting, of being shown up as a fraud, must have transmitted itself to them. Insofar as I was afraid to be exposed; they too would be afraid.

This moment was the seed from which my teaching grew from that time on, though it didn't feel like growth, but more like being pushed from behind by a force I couldn't see and whose name I didn't know. The first change came by accident.

One autumn, early in my time at Duke, I knew I wouldn't be able to prepare my classes in the usual way (I had agreed to give lectures at five different places and had to write some of them from scratch), so I borrowed from a colleague a method she called "no-frills" teaching. What the method boiled down to was this: the students were responsible for presenting the material to the class for most of the semester. I'd make up the syllabus and explain it in detail at the beginning of the course and try to give most of my major ideas away. (This was hard, since holding onto my ideas in case I should need them later was bred in the bone after twenty-odd years in the classroom.) The students would sign up for two topics on the syllabus that interested them and work with whoever else had signed up for their topic; anywhere from two to four people would be in charge on any given day. I'd meet with the groups beforehand to discuss their ideas and strategies of presentation, and afterward I'd offer them feedback.

The first presentation given this way was on the film *Gunfight at the O.K. Corral*. It was my first Westerns course, and the students were mostly men. A change came over the atmosphere of the class: it was almost like being at a football game. The students abounded in energy and ideas. There was a good-natured rough-and-tumble about the discussion. The whole class got involved. What a treat! The students were doing all the work, and their discussion of the film was just as interesting and valuable as mine would have been. It was a revelation.

From this point forward my classes were more alive than they'd ever been before. More students took part in discussions, they talked more to each other and less to me, and the intensity and quality of their engagement with the course material was gratifying. Not having the burden of responsibility for how things went every time, I could pay attention to what was being said, to who was talking, to how things felt in the class, and I could contribute when I had something really important to say. I did less work and enjoyed class more. Amazing!

But I felt guilty. How could something so easy be any good? I was possessed by an ingrained belief that only backbreaking work could produce excellent results, and that it must be selfish to teach in a way that was pleasurable and free from fear. In shifting the burden of performance onto the students, wasn't I making them do work I was too lazy to do myself? What were they paying me for? Yet while it was true that sometimes they couldn't deal with the material as well as I could, that was why they needed to grapple with it. It wasn't important for me to polish my skills, but they did need to develop theirs. Besides, after a while I found, uncannily, that my students knew what I was thinking even when I hadn't said anything. And their presentations were getting better and better. The second time I taught the Westerns course a student group produced an hour-long video criticizing violence in film. It was one of the most stunning presentations I've ever seen.

After these classes I could never teach in the old way again. I could never fool myself into believing that what *I* had to say was ultimately more important to the students than what *they* thought and felt. I had learned that each student was a walking field of energy teeming with agendas. I had to conduct my classes so as to tap into that energy field and elicit those agendas. There was no road back. Besides, once I had tasted the thrill of being together with students in a class instead of being all alone up there in front, I wanted more. I wanted to let go of everything that separated me from the other people in the room. I wanted to know them, I wanted them to know each other, and I wanted them to discover themselves.

———

"When you come right down to it," Picasso said in 1932, "all you have is your self. Your self is a sun with a thousand rays in your belly. The rest is nothing." I'm not sure about "The rest is nothing," but Picasso is right about the self being all you have. In learning to listen to myself I had embarked on a journey where maps and compasses got in the way rather than pointing it out, and an inner radar took over, leading me to places that used to be off-limits. In the realm of teaching this meant going outside the classroom, into the students' lives, into unknown subject matter, into my own psyche. For the "no-frills" method was only the beginning.

I began to teach courses where there was no syllabus—just some readings I'd put together in order to set the stage for the students to take over. I felt myself metamorphosing into a person I'd never met before. I would sit on the floor of my study where I meditated every morning, and every morning a column of fear would rise up inside me. I never knew what was going to happen in my classes. What had begun as a concern for what was going on inside my students' heads at the beginning of class had turned into a large-scale taking apart of everything I had ever done in my teaching life. It was an avalanche, a hemorrhage; whatever it was, I couldn't stop it. Like the animals in the title of Yeats's poem "The Circus Animals' Desertion," the positions I held, my main ideas, my interpretations of texts, exited. Not that I didn't still believe in them, but I could no longer impose my ideas on students, for that was what talking in class on some preassigned topic seemed like to me. There was, I felt, no knowledge apart from the situation. All I could do was respond; I couldn't prepare. I could only be in a state of preparedness. Everything became a throw of the dice. I called it teaching nothing.

I simultaneously thought of myself as a fraud—someone passing for a teacher who didn't in fact have anything to teach—and as a real person for the first time in my life. Not that the previous situations I'd occupied as a teacher had been false; they were simply different. When I thought I had knowledge to impart, I really was imparting something. But my situation had changed. I no longer needed or wanted to be validated in a certain way, validated by the authority of knowledge and expertise, by the experience of being the one who talks while others listen. I wanted to be in the moment. And to be there, I couldn't have a program, or a prepared text, a thing that I put in between me and whatever was happening. Between me and the students. The thing—knowledge, whatever—would get in the way.

122

Get in the way of what? you may ask, quite reasonably. *Isn't the teacher supposed to put something out there for the students to grasp? Isn't she supposed to tell them things? Or, more exaltedly, provide a structure within which or upon which their own thinking can work?* That would be one way. But the way that appealed to me then, that called and coerced me (for this was not a choice, really, it was what I had to do), was to have no knowledge. To know nothing, nothing solid, pre-existing, nothing that would deflect the course of events from its unpredictable path. I thought of myself, as I taught those courses, as waiting, like the scholar-gypsy in Matthew Arnold's poem, for the spark from heaven to alight, to feel the *atman*, the breath, brushing by my cheek. I wanted to be fully aware of what was happening and not speaking words that would prevent the spirit from being heard.

I got to the point where the students supplied the course material themselves and all I did to prepare for class was make cookies or buy Danish, make coffee, bring fruit, be sure there were enough napkins, and see to it that the mechanics of the course were taken care of—give directions to where we would meet off-campus, organize the writing groups, call people who'd been absent.

What would I do next? Not show up at all? I started comparing myself to King Lear. Afraid of finding myself barefoot, and living at the mercy and pleasure of others, day by day growing more of a stranger to myself and my friends, until finally I would be out there on the heath, shorn of everything, alone, in the howling gale. *Blow, winds, and crack your cheeks! rage, blow!*

Even I have to smile at this, sitting at my computer inside my comfortable house. Let's face it, I wasn't going to blow away. But the definition of the "nothing" experience is that you don't know whether it's going to turn out all right or not.

———

All this is by way of transcribing an inner history that had its outward manifestation in the conduct of some classes I taught. Its significance doesn't lie in these classes primarily, but in the observation that if you empty yourself out and don't fill the space, something will arise. If you can become quiet even for only a few moments, if you can get out of your own way, if your cup can become empty momentarily, it can be filled.

If the cup is empty, it can be filled.

I read this saying in the diary of a woman who was training with a Sufi master, and it summarizes both aspects of the narrative I'm trying to convey, the inner life and the outward practice. The moment of emptiness and terror had to occur. It was a death preliminary to the start of something.

———

My childhood friends, Mary Ellen and Betty Ann Hayes, had showed up every year sometime around March with a smudge on their foreheads. I wanted one, too. The ashes on the forehead, along with holy water, making the sign of the cross, first communion, bowing your head at the name of Jesus, and saying the rosary, set them apart in a way that made them belong. Something *claimed* them; what it was I didn't really know, some hocus-pocus. All I knew was that I wanted to be part of it, too, not left standing alone, like the cheese in "The Farmer in the Dell."

The desire not to be alone in my classes led to much of what I did by way of experiment. That and the longing to be free from fear. I say this now, in retrospect; at the time I just did things, impelled by a force unnameable.

There was one class I took notes on (because I was so frightened) that achieved the kind of atmosphere I was aiming for without knowing it.

Each student presented to the class the material he or she was most interested in—the heart of a senior thesis, early dissertation research, a book that was crucial to the student's life; we read the assigned material beforehand, and the student whose week it was talked and lead the discussion. The point was for the student to discover what his or her emotional investment in the subject was, to find out why, out of all the topics in the world, he or she had picked this one to work on. Then, when the presentation was over, all the students wrote to the presenter describing their reactions to the material, to the class discussion, to what the person had said. This "method" worked itself out *ambulando*. It didn't exist the first day we met, or the second or the third or the fourth. It took about four weeks to work it out.

The class had a quality that other classes I'd known had not had. When someone spoke, it wasn't just an idea thrown into the discussion, it was a human voice, a person being heard like a bell whose timbre is unreproducible. A particular tone, a particular resonance, Leigh—the senior on the women's basketball team—direct, honest, clear-eyed; Amelia, the gracious African-American woman with a degree from North Carolina Central, stylishly dressed, soft-voiced, gentle, a practicing Buddhist who shared her mantra with us; Professor Goto, a visiting professor of American literature from a university in Japan, deeply sensitive, charming, willing to enter into our ways, who invited the whole class to dinner before he left. The people in this class would shine, one after another, when we met. What I saw, when I went to class, was their beauty.

After the first couple of weeks, we started meeting at the apartment of one of the students, on Tuesday afternoons. The feeling of the apartment—it was attractive, cozy, cheerful—provided an atmosphere in which certain things could happen and others couldn't, or didn't. We became more sociable, relaxed, chummier. Carrie, our hostess, a divinity student who was wheelchair-bound, kept birds, and sometimes one of them flew around or the others made noise, providing a kind of healthy diversion that didn't get in the way of our discussions but made them saner, a reminder of the ongoingness of the world.

Meeting in the apartment on Tuesdays changed the character of the Thursday class. We still had a special aura that we carried from the apartment. It wasn't just another class anymore; it was *this* class. After we began meeting at Carrie's I began bringing food; often I'd bake something—brownies, corn bread, a loaf of bread, once a cake—or, if I didn't have time, I'd buy something on the way to school or bring fruit and cookies from home. Sometimes students contributed—Amelia brought a chocolate mousse cake to celebrate her fiftieth birthday; Leanne brought cookies her aunt had made; Carrie made brownies. The food helped create an atmosphere. There was an element of caring, of concern for the body, of extra credit, so to speak, being distributed to the group freely.

What characterized the course in the end was absence of pressure, of the very fear that had been so present at the outset, when several students dropped the course and we floundered and fumbled our way toward a content and a design. I felt relaxed in class and in preparing for class. I knew something interesting would come forth no matter what. We had a quiet confidence in each other, confidence that something valuable would emerge. No one at anybody's throat, but many points of view nonetheless. Was this the peaceable kingdom? I don't know.

In the case at hand, I wasn't sure we had achieved the maximum in quality, whatever that would be. Perhaps toward the end we became a little too passive. It's hard to say. But that sort of judgment seems inappropriate. Each class is different; that's part of the point. Each class has its potentialities and its limitations. You do what you can within the situation; you are, collectively, what you are. Each class a concelebration, a holy communion, of sorts.

———

When I talk this way about my classes, people often think I'm criticizing them. If they're professors, they think I don't respect the way they teach. If they're not professors but have gone to college, they think I'm criticizing the education they got. If they didn't go to college, they think I must be crazy. *What is college for if not for learning what the professor knows about the subject? Otherwise why go? Isn't this way of teach-*

ing awfully self-centered? people ask. *Isn't what you're talking about something like . . . group therapy?* they say, voices tinged with suspicion; the phrase "touchy-feely" is not far behind. "Practicing psychiatry without a license" someone threw at me once. I look over my shoulder. Are they right? Doubt is in the road.

Yet I believe that school should be a safe place, the way home is supposed to be. A place where you belong, where you can grow and express yourself freely, where you know and care for the other people and are known and cared for by them, a place where people come before information and ideas. School needs to comprehend the relationship between the subject matter and the lives of students, between teaching and the lives of teachers, between school and home.

"Fear," Krishnamurti wrote, "fear is what prevents the flowering of the mind."

———

It is Christmas, 1958. I have come home from college and am having Christmas dinner with my family. Sitting across the table from me is Delly DeLaguna, formerly a professor of philosophy at Bryn Mawr College, now retired. She, along with her daughter Freddy, a professor of anthropology at Bryn Mawr, are dinner guests at my parents' house, friends of my parents. Delly has just asked me a penetrating question about my studies (I am a sophomore at Bryn Mawr), and I am about to answer. I think I have been talking about T. S. Eliot, and she has asked what I like about him or what I find important. I no longer remember the exact question, but I get up from the table to remove a dish, and on the way into the kitchen I pause by her chair and recite the following lines from *The Family Reunion:* "You are the consciousness of your unhappy family, its bird sent flying through the purgatorial flame."

As the lines came out, I felt a sudden twinge; I had an uneasy sense that they *might have been inappropriate*, or *might have been misinterpreted* by others at the table. In truth I do not think I had any notion at all that they expressed what I felt about myself and my parents and my general life situation. I honestly believed I was making a literary judgment, innocent and high-minded, exhibiting both my taste and Eliot's profundity. I do remember, though, that there was a moment of silence from which I escaped by passing through the swinging doors into the kitchen.

That moment can stand as well as any other for the lesson I'm trying to teach myself. It is the moment I want most to avoid: unconsciously reenacting on a public stage an inward drama of which I have no knowledge.

I sit down and reread *Ash-Wednesday* after all these years, and it speaks to me in a new way. Some internal change has helped me to sympathize with the poet instead of hating him for what I took to be his lack of feeling. Eliot's experience of spiritual death, the day of ashes that precedes a longed for resurrection, is something I can respond to without knowing exactly what it means. I feel him swing between a complete undoing of himself—his bones scattered in the desert, himself forgotten—and the first starting up of hope. "This is the time of tension between dying and birth," Ash Wednesday, everything gone, and you just waiting—I have some sense now of what that might be. The poet is praying for himself. His poem is an act of surrender, a whispered hope of forgiveness; in the end the poet is not afraid to turn and ask for help.

> Sister, mother
> And spirit of the river, spirit of the sea,
> Suffer me not to be separated
>
> And let my cry come unto Thee.

It's the suffering that attracts me to this poem, as it attracted me in my sophomore year when I suffered and didn't know it. If only Miss

Woodworth had said something about that, had encouraged us to speak of what we felt as we read it, instead of trying to sound knowledgeable about literature. I look back through my cerulean blue hardback copy of T. S. Eliot, *The Complete Poems and Plays, 1909–1950* and the notes I've made in the margins of *The Waste Land* are so literal, they make me want to cry. Next to the phrase "a broken Coriolanus," I've written, "Symbol of proud idealism." Next to "Burning burning burning burning," I've written "Lust—an image used by both Buddha and St. Augustine." What did I know? It was terribly confusing, lines in Greek, in Sanskrit, in German, in Latin. I even *knew* Italian and still didn't understand the references to Dante. Those were desperate times, understanding T. S. Eliot in college—you had to be able to do that if you were an English major. So I wrote down the dry bits of information the teacher gave us; it was like eating dog kibble. "These fragments I have shored against my ruins," Eliot writes near the end of the poem. That was me.

But it's possible to understand the poetry at another level without knowing what the references mean. It's possible to interrogate your soul and learn from its cries and whispers what the poet might be saying. Oh, I read Eliot, all right. I read him with my heart, and what I understood was appalling. But I couldn't admit to myself or articulate what I had seen. Turning back now to "The Hollow Men," looking at those dead lines, I see what they say, and I can hardly take it. Irony of ironies, it was Eliot who was able to bare his heart in verse, in death's dream kingdom. But the reality was too much to bear for my teachers, for me, so we lost ourselves in explication. We said: these lines are from Kyd's *Spanish Tragedy*; these are from Gerard de Nerval. "Those are pearls that were his eyes," a reference to Shakespeare.

What I see in Eliot now is what I saw in him then but couldn't acknowledge, the suffering. It was personal; it was long-drawn-out; it was unappetizing. A lot of sickness in Eliot, old unresolved fears and longings, half-formulated desires, unacknowledged hatred, and paralyzing despair. His innards are half rotted; they send up a kind of stink that curls between the lines but is denied. You can talk about the sources in the *Purgatorio* while secretly identifying with his crucifixion. Reading his poetry was a way of experiencing something without letting yourself know you were experiencing it. The morbid fantasizing of unhappy intellectuals under the guise of doing literary criticism.

"Weave, weave the sunlight in your hair."

My relation to Eliot's fear and sickness is different now mainly because I know how I feel when I read the poetry, whereas before I couldn't let myself know. He says in *The Waste Land*, commanding us: "Come in under the shadow of this red rock . . ./[And] I will show you fear in a handful of dust." I obeyed. For years in an attempt to brighten grim surroundings, I had a cheap red rug in my university office, and I would say to myself upon entering, like an automatic reflex, "Come in under the shadow of this red rug," but never the second line, about fear, which I'd forgotten, since I lived it every day. Afraid that my classes wouldn't go well, afraid that my students wouldn't like me, afraid that my senior colleagues wouldn't think well of me. Living under the shadow of this red rug was hard to do!

My fear of my students and of my colleagues was after all a fear of myself. The same shape twisted on the bannister. If I could have read Eliot in full consciousness of what I was feeling as a freshman, as a sophomore, I could have begun to face myself. But instead I was like the character at the beginning of *The Waste Land* who, only vaguely aware of her disease, says, "I read, much of the night, and go south in winter." I knew I was like that woman and that her reading and her vacations were a defeat. Half hearted, polite, well behaved.

Who would have thought death had undone so many?

The lines from Eliot return without asking. I hated them and loved them at the same time, perversely esoteric and full of unacknowledged pain. *"Sovegna vos a temps de ma dolor"* Eliot writes in a footnote to *The Waste Land*. He is playing hide-and-seek, quoting a line from Dante, who is quoting a line in Provençal spoken by a soul burning in Purgatory: "While there's still time, remember my pain." Remember my pain. This was the poet's message after all.

Now that I've recaptured the emotions that reading poetry arouses, I hardly know how to teach it. My stock has gone down to zero, and nothing that I know seems to do me any good. In relation to literature, the ostensible subject of my expertise, I feel a little like Prufrock at the end:

> We have lingered in the chambers of the sea
> By sea-girls wreathed with seaweed red and brown
> Till human voices wake us, and we drown.

10
———

THE DAY

I WALKED OUT

OF CLASS

Over a period of six years, I taught seven courses under the no-frills method and eight in which I pushed further into the unknown. While I was teaching the more experimental courses my life was a roller coaster. I'd go to bed at night, obsessed with thoughts of what had happened in class that day. The teaching was not an orderly progression through a body of material. It was not about the mastery of knowledge or the acquisition of a skill. It was about letting chaos in, about not knowing, not being in control.

Early on I'd stumbled on the realization that my students had very little idea who they were. My idea was to give them the opportunity to find out. I wouldn't tell them what to think or what to do. I would let them flounder and make them take the responsibility for learning on themselves. Since they had no experience of this, naturally, once the door to self-determination was open, chaos entered. How long it stayed depended on the class—sometimes a few weeks, sometimes as many as six or seven. Then the course would settle down. A plan would be produced, assignments given, routines established.

Each course I taught this way was different and had its own history of surprises and disappointments, moments of revelation, frustration, and

132

joy. When I ask myself what the value was of teaching in this way, what the students learned, what I learned, my throat closes and I fall silent. It's not so much that the questions don't have answers as that the answers can't be given in a straightforward way. Occasionally, when a student in one of these classes would report that his or her roommate had asked what the course was like, the student's reply invariably would be, "You had to be there." And it's true, you did. The most I can say by way of summation is that for me the courses were of such an intensity that I am still trying to understand them, as if they were written in burning cipher, and I have not yet discovered the code.

One incident that remains branded in my consciousness occurred about a third of the way through a course called Reading for Yourself, my most experimental course thus far. I had come to class that day loaded for bear. We had been discussing some very short texts—some poems, a couple of short stories—assigned by one of the students, and the poems (by Emily Dickinson) had come from a movie we'd seen together, which they'd also chosen. But not all the students seemed to have read the material; not all were participating by a long shot. I'd bent over backward to give them the chance to do what *they* wanted to do, and their response had been constrained, awkward, even in some cases listless. I'd been feeling frustrated for some time, but by that point I was mad. I came to class that day prepared to walk out if *something* didn't happen.

I made a speech. I talked about how I'd tried to let them take the lead, and how disappointed I was that people weren't more engaged. I said that when I came to class I was one hundred percent *there*, and that I expected them to be too. I said I felt frustrated and badly treated by them. I said I was fed up. Well, there was an awful silence. And then one student, her name was Shannon, spoke up. She'd been one of the silent ones, a tall blonde half-drowsy outdoorsy girl who looked sometimes as if she were thinking thoughts of her own that she definitely did not wish to share.

Shannon said: "I hate to read."

I was stunned. There followed a shouting match between the two of us in which I asked her what in hell she was doing at Duke University, to which she replied that it was that or work at McDonald's. These words and the ensuing exchange made such a deep impression on me that my thinking about undergraduate education since has been largely based on it. But at the moment, I was still mad at the students for not putting more of themselves into the course, and at a certain point I gathered up my things, said it was up to them to come up with a plan for the rest of the semester, and left.

I got in my car and drove to Main Street and paused: it was a beautiful day, and I had my dog, Ribbon, in the car, and my lunch. I'd heard about this entrance to the paths along the Eno River that I'd never been to before, so . . . I decided, what the hell, and off I went. I could have gone back to my office and worked on the tenure letter I'd been laboring over for the last couple of days, or answered some of the endless mail, but it seemed pusillanimous. If I was asking for courage and spontaneity from the students, the least I could do was ask the same of myself.

To get to the Eno you go out Hillsborough Road, cross Route 85, and before you know it, Cole Mill Road comes up on your right. You take Cole Mill for quite a ways—through Croasdaile where some of the wealthy people of Durham live. You keep on going and going until you pass an ammo and guns store on the right, and not too long after that, a road called Rivermont. Then the road dips down, there's a sign for the river, and the next left is the turn-in for the Eno River State Park.

If you take the path to the river, at first you can hardly see it. You only get glimpses through the trees, as if the river were hiding, veiling itself. The trees had very small leaves and looked delicate and graceful; they were lightly touched with yellow and trailing their branches, for it was the fall of the year. The river was grassy at first, and flowing swiftly, brownish, with lots of bubbles. It looked alive. I walked until I came to a rocky beach where the sun was, and I sat down and thought about the class. I'd been making speeches to myself the whole way out, coming up with wonderful pithy sentences I could have said if I'd thought of them at the time. I sat on the stones, arms around my legs, while Ribbon enjoyed herself in the water, nose down, smelling things, ears perking up at sounds she could hear and I couldn't, and I speechified some more in my head until finally I started thinking about Shannon.

"Shannon," I said, "the only person who gets a Pass," I said, dramatically, "because she spoke the truth," I said, eyes big, glowering at them all, mentally. But then I thought, what could Shannon have done other than go to Duke? Really and concretely. Well, let's see, I mused. How do I see Shannon? Probably out of doors. I see her on a sailboat, a large sailboat, on the ocean. She's the owner of the boat, and she takes people on vacations in the Pacific or the South Seas. The scene shifts. Now Shannon is tramping through the woods collecting samples, rocks or ferns. She's some kind of environmentalist, and this is part of her work. (I admit she'd have to have gone to some sort of college for that.) She has on muddy boots and a neat hat. Another change. This time Shannon is indoors, her tall figure gracefully inclined so that a little girl with long curly black hair can explain the picture she's been making with finger paints. Shannon is an art teacher in the schools of East Los Angeles. She's wearing jeans, and she's very happy. But, perhaps happier still, there she is in the same jeans, only this time standing with a pitchfork in her hand and wearing a straw hat; the hillside she's on is in Northern California, and she's on her farm, the one she finally bought. She's having trouble with something mechanical, but her troubles are only the froth on a deep sense of satisfaction and accomplishment. One final picture. I couldn't resist it: Shannon on safari in Africa. This time the hat is a topi, and she has a lot of camera gear slung over her shoulders. She is wearing a tan outfit and looking beautiful.

"Far-fetched? Maybe, but all possible. And you"—I'm still speaking to the students in my head—"you wouldn't have to go to a four-year high-pressure traditional university for any of them. You could take sailing lessons, get a job in a marina, crew for a friend. You could go to art school. You could apprentice yourself to a farmer. I had a friend who dropped out of an M.A. program in history, apprenticed himself to a farmer in Bucks County, Pennsylvania, and then borrowed the money to buy himself a dairy farm. He made a go of it and became quite well-to-do breeding cattle, but his family fell apart—another story. Anyway, you get the point. The choices are not just a B.A. from Duke or working at McDonald's. I'm not trying to get you to drop out of school, either. It's just that we get afraid that if we don't take the road well travelled, we'll go nowhere."

(Still talking to them, still preaching, I can't help myself.) "And at the risk of sounding incredibly corny, as Holden Caulfield would say"—we'd just read *Catcher in the Rye*—"let me confess that as I was driving out here to the Eno a famous line from *Hamlet* popped into my head, a line I'd been taught to regard as a pious platitude. It's Polonius's advice to his son. Holden mentions it disparagingly in *Catcher.*

> This above all: to thine own self be true,
> And it must follow, as the night the day,
> Thou canst not then be false to any man.

That was what I was doing when I said I felt you were holding out on me; I was trying to be true to myself. And that is what I want you to do."

I sent this inner speech to my students in the form of a paper entitled "Shannon's Choice." I had walked out of class on a Thursday. The following weekend was parents' weekend at Duke. I imagined some irate parent calling the dean on Monday morning and demanding his money back because his son or daughter was in a class where the instructor had not only demanded that the students organize their own course, but had actually walked out on them. I imagined a lawsuit being brought against me by parents, the university. I imagined being called on the carpet by the powers that be.

None of this came to pass. When I got to my office Monday afternoon, there was a huge pile of Xeroxes outside my door, and taped to the wall was a long complicated list of assignments and responsibilities the students promised to carry out. I was overjoyed and limp with relief. I made a card out of four pieces of colored paper with "Hurray!" written all over it again and again. It's still taped to the wall beside my desk, a reminder to me that some experiments, anyway, do turn out.

———

Or do they?

The one thing I've learned from doing experimental teaching is that you never know, really, what you've accomplished. You never know what the students have learned, or if they've learned anything, anything solid. One student in this class bought a guitar at the end of the semester and learned to play it. That was the kind of outcome the course had. Another student signed up for a semester at sea (it was Shannon). At a party at my house at the end of the semester I asked the students why they thought it was that we had never succeeded in talking about literature (we had done all sorts of things in that class but rarely had a good literary discussion). They said it was because they didn't know how.

I felt terrible. I had failed to teach them how to talk about literature! But then I stopped myself. They also told me—several students did— that their ancient love of reading had been rekindled, and others said they had begun to enjoy reading for the first time. Because, they said, the atmosphere was relaxed and nonpressuring. Some students had started reading things on their own who had never done that before. That was learning, but not the kind I was used to aiming for, so I hardly recognized it. It was a change in behavior.

As a group we had reached the point where we could have begun to devote ourselves to a serious intellectual pursuit, because by that time we trusted each other to a significant degree. We had done the work of learning how to be together as a class, had satisfied our curiosity, and had established ourselves as accepted, as contributing, members of the group. The discussion we had at my house that night at the end of the semester was one of our few sustained serious conversations. It was excellent. People spoke from a fairly deep level within themselves. They didn't need to impress anyone, me or the other students, because all that had been gotten through, and, besides, it was all over now. Tonally, the conversation was perfect.

If I had been able to have those students for another semester, what would I have done? They were at the point where they were *asking* me to teach them about literature. But what would I have wanted to teach them? I truly do not know. And if I did know, how would I go about doing it in a way that would not bring about a regression from the level of trust and honesty we had reached with one another? Another question I had about this course was, could the floundering, the fear, the chaos and shilly-shallying that characterized the beginning have been avoided? Yes, of course it could. The question is not could it have been avoided, but *should* it have been avoided? This is a real question for me and one I cannot answer.

As for myself, what I learned in this course didn't surface until later. It wasn't until I was getting ready to design a new course in American literature that I knew what I had learned in Reading for Yourself. It came to me in an image: an image of one of the students, his name was Ben, standing on the table in our classroom, holding a sword of light over his head.

How did this happen? One day I gave the students an assignment I'd invented on the spur of the moment in one of my earliest experimental classes: to go to Toys "R" Us. We drove over in three or four cars, spent forty-five minutes in the store—the rules were no talking to anyone, and you could only buy one thing—and we came back to the classroom and wrote for the remainder of the period. For next time, everyone finished the writing assignment, to write eight pages on what the Toys "R" Us experience had brought up.

Ben had bought one of those swords that lights up when you move it, an imitation of the laser swords of the Jedi knights in the *Star Wars* trilogy. When we came back to the class, people were clowning around, and Ben climbed up on the table and said, "Oh, Captain, my Captain." His getting up on the table and reciting poetry was his reference to another assignment we'd done, which was to see *Dead Poets Society* and discuss it together the next day. In the course of that discussion—the best we ever had in that class—it became clear that we were talking about ourselves. I was Robin Williams, the rebel teacher, whom the students called "Captain," and who they stood up for—literally, they stood on their desks—when he was fired from the school. Part of the class was against Robin Williams's philosophy of self-expression and self-determination, and part of the class was for it. That day, one of the students brought to class the same poetry anthology that had been used in the movie, the one from which the students read to each other in the cave where their society met. My students wanted to read poetry aloud, too. They found the poems from the movie—I remember their reading lines like "My name is Ozymandias, king of kings," "Oh, Captain, my Captain, our fearful trip is done"—grabbing the book out of one another's hands, they were so eager to have a turn. (In all my years of teaching, I'd never seen anything like this.) As they read—and they read poorly, having never been taught how to read poetry aloud—a chill went down my spine, and I felt gooseflesh all over my body. It was the chill you get sometimes from reading poetry. On another day, we read aloud a poem from another movie we'd seen—*Sophie's Choice*—a poem about death by Emily Dickinson that is recited twice in the movie. As the semester unfolded, that poem kept going through my head. One day I decided to see whether the students knew it too, so I put it on the board with some words missing. It turned out that many of them did know it. We recited it together, as a class. I felt the chill again.

When I created my new American literature course, I did so with the sole intention of letting the students feel the thrilling power of words. In Reading for Yourself, the teaching function had been reversed, at least as far as learning about literature was concerned. My students had reintroduced me to the magic of poetry, and I felt for the first time in a long, long time the enchantment that had originally led me to the study of literature, an enchantment that is summed up for me in the image of Ben standing on the table with his sword of light. Somehow, something precious had been rekindled; I didn't want to let the flame die out.

———

Because I was doing this experimenting alone, without colleagues who'd taken similar risks, and had no way to compare my experience to the experiences of others, I needed some way to come to terms with what I was doing. I needed some way to make sense of experiences that were overpowering in their intensity. So when an invitation came to talk to some undergraduates at Eckerd College, in St. Petersburg, Florida, who were preparing to go into college teaching, I took the opportunity to put the course into narrative form, hoping by this means to lay its ghost.

But narrative did not suit. Thrilling episodes came out sounding banal; the roller-coaster adventure became a pedestrian recital of events. This kind of teaching seemed to require a new kind of writing, a form that would reflect the spasmodic, concentrated quality of the experience, its precariousness, the constant sense of teetering on the brink that accompanied me from day one of that course and during most of my experimental courses, only letting go of me now and then.

11

POSTCARDS

FROM THE EDGE

· 1 ·

Dear Fellow Teachers,

What do you do when silence breaks out in your class, the times when you suddenly forget everything you were going to say, or you ask a question no one answers, and you sit there wishing you were dead, blush rising from the throat, face hot, throat clenched?

Last semester when I tried to hand authority over to my students, we had many such moments. Often we just sat there looking at each other. I nearly died, and so did they.

Yet living through those silences taught me something. They had a bonding effect, like living through a war. As a result of this experience I've come to think pain and embarrassment are not the worst things for a class. At least the moments are real. At least everyone feels intensely. At least everyone is *there*.

What do you think?

Jane

· 2 ·

Poem Postcard

No monuments record the bravery of teachers,
Or tell our conquered fears,
There is no Tomb of the Unknown Teacher,
No surgery for our scars.

All our injuries are internal.
No one counts the pain,
Least of all the teachers.
We go sightless on.

To teach is to be battered,
Scrutinized, and drained,
Day after day. We know this.
Still, it is never said.

What it is to be up there
Exposed to the hostile gaze
Will never be told by teachers—
The knowledge is too much.

· 3 ·

Dear All-wise, Imagined Mentor,

My class had suffered together. Its members had gotten to know each other. People had taken risks. Something like authenticity had begun to mark the level of exchange. But whenever we tried to talk about literature, authenticity would fly out the window. Our talk seemed forced, desultory.

One day, to break the ice (again), we played Pictionary, a game like charades, only you draw instead of acting. We screamed, we jumped up

142

and down, laughed, were intensely quiet. There was total concentration, participation, self-forgetfulness.

Then we switched gears. For the last twenty minutes people read aloud their assignments—what they thought Holden Caulfield did after the end of *Catcher in the Rye*. Silence descended; it was the living and the dead. This happened over and over. It was as if, given the opportunity to choose between literature and life, or rather, between literature and each other, we chose each other. The class never did learn how to discuss a literary text, though we fell into a habit of reading poetry aloud from time to time.

What could we have done to avoid this quandary?

Should it have been avoided?

Wondering, in Durham

· 4 ·

[To Parker Palmer, a leader in higher education reform and author of *To Know as We Are Known: A Spirituality of Education*]

Dear Parker,

When I began paying attention to students, I stopped caring about knowledge. Knowledge, for me, became something "over there—Behind the Shelf," as in the line from the Dickinson poem:

> I cannot live with You—
> It would be Life—
> And Life is over there—
> Behind the Shelf

If knowledge is "over there—Behind the Shelf," life is right in front of me in the classroom, in the faces and bodies of the students. *They* are life, and I want us to share our lives, make something together, for as long as the course lasts, and let that be enough.

143

I think the thing I'm aiming for is a sense of the classroom as sacramental. The class experience itself becomes the end and aim of education. Not something learned that you can take away from the class, not a skill, or even a perspective on the world, but an experience worth having as it goes by, moment by moment. I'm really looking for somebody to give me permission to think these things. Will you do it?

Love,
Jane

· 5 ·

Dear Students,

When I pay attention to the subject matter in class, instead of to you, I get excited, think of an idea that just *has* to be said, blurt it out, and, more often than not, kill something. As in the Dickinson poem

My life had stood
A loaded gun
In corners

when I speak the report is so loud it deafens. No one can hear anything but what I've said. Discussion dies. It seems it's either you or me, my authority or your power to speak. What do I do that shuts people up? Or is this a false dilemma? Help!

Sincerely,
Jane

· 6 ·

To I Don't Know Who:

Sometimes the feelings I have toward my students are romantic. It's like being in love. You know how when you're in love or have a crush on somebody, you're always looking forward to the next meeting with desire and trepidation—will he or she be glad to see me? Will he or she be late? not come at all? Will she or he think I'm smart? good-looking? a nice person? It's the roller-coaster of love—up one day and down the next—no two classes the same. How soon will we be going steady? Will our love be true? Do you love me like I love you?

Am I the only person who feels this way about teaching?

Wondering, in Durham

· 7 ·

[This postcard is addressed to the registrar at Duke University, whose name is Harry Demik.]

Dear Mr. Demik,

Last semester I stopped giving letter grades in my courses and got into trouble with your office. There were mix-ups regarding both classes, rules against what I was doing, but things got straightened out, and I didn't have to give grades.

Grades, of course, are judgments. Judgments rendered by One Who Knows. The way I teach now, judgment seems inappropriate—judgment of the students by the instructor, or of the instructor by the students, or even of the whole course by all its members. I offered these courses Pass/Fail for a reason: you can't grade a person's soul.

Of course, toward the end of the semester, as the pressure from their other courses mounts, the students in my courses slack off, and then I feel put out. I have no solution for this problem.

Jane Tompkins

· 8 ·

To Whom It May Concern:

I cleared a pile of newspapers from the kitchen table in order to write this postcard, but on top of the pile a section on hunger and homelessness caught my eye. There were terrible statistics, such as forty thousand children die in the world every day from starvation. The lead sentence in one article read: "The longest journey a person can take is the twelve inches from the head to the heart."

Who is helping our students to make this journey?

Wondering, in Durham

· 9 ·

Nightmare Postcard

Dear Professor Tompkins,

I've read your article, and I think you're fooling yourself. You're cheating your students under the guise of liberating them. These students need guidance; they need a model. They need to hear books discussed boldly, rigorously, with discipline, and in a spirit of inquiry. They're only eighteen or nineteen; they don't know how to be intellectuals. It's your job to show them, and you're not doing it. You ought to be fired.

Disgusted

· 10 ·

Dear Disgusted,

You may be right. But twisting in my seat, looking away in an agony of frustration, staring down at the desk, and taking deep breaths, I've learned to curb my impulse to correct the students, to show them the way, because when I do it shuts them up. Allowed to meander to its furthest most insignificant trickle, ending in a long moment of emptiness, or allowed to reach a pinnacle of disorderly, excited hilarity and confusion, a class discussion can give birth to the moment that changes the destiny of the course. The student too afraid to speak up at any other time may step into that moment of silence; or the giddiness of the atmosphere

146

may produce an insight, a wild metaphorical leap of the imagination on someone's part that crystallizes everything. Then there's the silence that attends the recognition of an important event. To me that precarious path is more precious than all the modelling in the world. Besides, they get that from their other professors.

Jane Tompkins

· 11 ·

Dear Jane,

Come on, now. You know this guy is onto something, but you're afraid to admit it. You just can't stand preparing for class anymore, so you get the students to do it. You can't stand the responsibility of making discussions work, so you opt out. You hand responsibility over to the students as a way of pretending to teach while really doing something else. Why not just quit?

Your Conscience

· 12 ·

To My Internalized Critic:

A class doesn't get to know itself until it has been let go. People's personalities won't be visible, their feelings and opinions won't surface, unless the teacher gets out of the way on a regular basis. You have to be willing to give up your authority, and the sense of identity and prestige that come with it, for the students to be able to feel their own authority. To get out of the students' way, the teacher has to learn how to get out of her own way. To not let her ego call the shots all the time. This is incredibly difficult. But I think it is a true path for a teacher.

Jane

147

· 13 ·

Dear C.,

Do you remember once we were having a telephone conversation about how busy we were? You were worrying about how you were ever going to finish the critical biography you'd been working like a dog on for years, we'd been talking about our families, when suddenly you burst out with: "I don't know what I would do. If my parents should die I wouldn't have time."

I'll never forget that moment, or the sound of your voice.

Jane

· 14 ·

Dear Friends,

I would have written you a letter instead of a postcard, but I didn't have time.

I wanted to tell you about what's happening in my life, but I didn't have time.

I would have invited you to dinner, but I didn't have time.

I would have done more reading before writing this paper, but I didn't have time.

We never got to cover the end of the novel because we ran out of time.

I would have read your article more carefully, but I didn't have time.

I didn't have time to read your article.

I wanted to call you, but I was afraid it would take too much time.

In haste,
Jane

· 15 ·

Dear Fellow Teachers:

In the classroom we say over and over that there's not enough time to do what we really want. But it's a lie. Listen to Mary Rose O'Reilley's reflection on this:

> Sister Teresa was past her prime, getting eccentric. She was supposed to teach us Art History from Prehistory to the Present. We spent weeks on primitive cave painting, then stalled on Giotto. Day after day, we sat in a dark classroom, looking at the confusion of spears and torches in "The Kiss of Judas"—until we knew it. Knew it. Later, lurking morosely in the positivist pews of Johns Hopkins University, where I read the Gospel of John in first year Greek, it was Giotto that rose before my eyes. That confusion of spears, and that alone, opened the Greek text to me. Now I knew two things.
>
> This nun having done her work, art stops short for me in the early fourteenth century. Somewhere, filed in some Platonic syllabus, lie Raphael's fat madonnas, but they are not for me: I do not know them. I suppose that is a loss. But I know two things.

So you see, whether or not you have enough time depends on what your conception of learning is.

Jane

· 16 ·

Dear Colleagues:

Here's a joke I remember from junior high school, or maybe it was college. A woman went to the doctor and said, "Doctor, I have this enormous desire to eat pancakes. I just can't get enough of them. What can

149

I do?" "Well," said the doctor, "that doesn't sound too serious. How many pancakes are we talking about?" "Oh," said the woman, "at home I have sixteen chests full."

When it comes to knowledge, we are like that woman. At home we have sixteen chests full, and we're dying to get our hands on sixteen more. But since even one cold pancake is too many, why are we doing this?

Jane

· 17 ·

[This postcard is to John Orr, my meditation teacher.]

Dear John,

I've begun to realize lately that I read as a reflex, to stuff my mind. It's too painful to remain conscious for very long at a time, attention free; even a fraction of the day is too much. So I read or write, talk or listen, watch TV, do a task that requires some degree of concentration; that way I can avoid the unpleasantness of open attention. Mainly it's reading I use to stanch the flow of unwanted mental events.

Love,
Jane

· 18 ·

[To my husband, Stanley Fish, a famous Milton scholar]

Dear Stan,

Remember the other day when I wanted you to spend time with me, and you said you had to work? I thought of Milton's sonnet on his blindness, and in particular, of this line: "God doth not need either man's work or his own gifts." *"God doth not need either man's work or his own gifts,"* I wanted to shout at you. *"His state is kingly. Thousands at his bidding speed and post o'er land and ocean without rest,"* so what the fuck are you doing working on your paper?

My whole life I never remembered these lines when *I* was busy. But still, I hope you take my point.

Love,
Jane

· 19 ·

[This postcard was written to the Ford Foundation Scholars at Eckerd College in St. Petersburg, Florida.]:

Dear Ford Foundation Scholars:

In the Political Correctness wars, where we fight over whether to teach *The Color Purple*, or what the First Amendment really means, we forget the weather. People's feelings get hurt; resentments build.

A friend of mine whose marriage was breaking up told me that how you deal with the problems that come up in a relationship is more important than what the problems are. It's the same in intellectual life. But we, your professors, do not know how to conduct ourselves when there is real conflict, inside the classroom or out. We fumble around. Sometimes we tear each other apart, or, afraid of doing that, we avoid speaking. I for one could use some instruction in how to disagree fruitfully. And in how to listen constructively to an opponent. I wish your generation would learn these skills and then teach them to us.

Hopefully,
Jane Tompkins

· 20 ·

Dear Teachers,

In school, it's students not books that are the important things. And the students are growing. And like other growing things, they need the right atmosphere to grow in. The atmosphere is what determines whether or not they will flourish. Of this atmosphere, books are only one part. What about the rest?

Do students get the sunshine of love and attention from their instructors? Do they receive the rain of affection and intimate exchange from one another? Do they have time and space to grow in?

J.T.

· 21 ·

[To Myself (from the future)]

Dear Jane,

Try not to worry so much about teaching. As you become more at peace with yourself, your classroom will become more peaceful. What is important is to carry your students in your heart, as you have begun to do.

Your inner guide

152

12

REVERIE

In my mind's eye I keep seeing rows. Rows of desks, running horizontal across a room, light yellow wooden tops, pale beige metal legs, a shallow depression for pencils at the far edge, and chairs of the same material, separate from the desks, movable. The windows—tall and running the length of the classroom—are on the left. Light streams through.

The rows are empty.

Now the desks darken and curve. They're made of older grainier wood; they're the kind with a surface that comes out from the back of the seat on your right and wraps around in front. The desk top is attached to the seat where you sit, which is clamped to the seats on either side or to those in front and in back. The desks metamorphose in my mind. Now they are hinged, tops brown and scarred; they open to reveal notebooks, textbooks covered in the shiny green-and-white book covers of Glen Rock Junior High; there's a bottle of mucilage and a pink eraser. On top, there's a hole for an inkwell, black and empty. The seat, when you stand, folds up behind.

Sometimes the desks are movable; more often they're clamped down. Always they're in rows. And empty. The teacher's place is empty, too, another desk, or tablelike thing. Sometimes it's a podium on a platform. The blackboard behind.

The scenes are all mixed together—grade school with graduate school—but always the windows along one side of the room, and always the desks in rows.

After babyhood we spend a lot of time learning to sit in rows. Going from unruly to ruled. Learning to write on pages that are lined. Learning to obey. There is no other way, apparently. Even if the desks were arranged in a circle, or were not desks at all but chairs or ottomans, still they would have to form some pattern. We would have to learn to sit still and listen.

The first part of life goes on for a long time. The habit of learning to sit in rows doesn't leave off when the rows themselves are gone. Having learned to learn the rules, you look for them everywhere you go, to avoid humiliation. You learn to find your seat in the invisible rows.

The last part of life, though, is different. It is no longer automatic, your walking in and sitting down. When you see a row, your gorge rises, or you are simply indifferent. When the command comes to be seated, you don't obey. All of a sudden, survival no longer depends on getting to your desk in the ten seconds after the buzzer sounds. It depends on listening only to your inner monitor, which says: You'd better go while the going's good. Time to give up the security of rows.

'Cause you're not *in* the classroom anymore. There is no blackboard with equations on it, no teacher with her pointer to point out what you need to know. No test, no assignment. No three o'clock when the bell for dismissal rings. No after school.

No smell of chalk dust and freshly sharpened pencils, no fragrances of different kinds of paper, gray and white and yellow, blank pages, lined and unlined, inviting you to prove something, yourself . . . I can do this problem, spell that word, name the capital of that country, explain the meaning of that term.

Though there was always fear associated with sitting in rows—am I too different? will I pass the test? does anybody like me?—the desks and chairs and tasks provided an escape from fear by giving me something definite to do. Add the column of figures. Learn the causes of the war.

Now, wandering the world outside of school, having transcended "rows," nothing to do, no place to go, I am terrified. In the huge, dark, unfurnished world without rows, I cower and tremble. Give me back Mrs. Colgan. Let me be in 1B again. Let me learn to add, to subtract, to carry and to borrow numbers. Give me a problem to do.

I see the light-filled classrooms, rows on rows, desks, chairs, waiting to be filled: let the lesson begin. "Our first assignment will be to learn the periodic table." Let me back in. Please. Let me sit down again, open my notebook to the first blank page, start writing. When is the exam?

13

KARATE LESSON

It was sometime after I had taught the course called Reading for Yourself where the students took over and did their own thing that I started to take karate. An offer of free classes for beginners in the month of June, from six to seven on Mondays and Wednesdays, seemed tempting. I thought perhaps if I mastered, or acquired some skill in, a martial art, the external competence would affect me internally, give me the ability to stand up for myself, to stop assuming all the power was on the other side, to meet confrontation firmly instead of avoiding it. After seven lessons I had learned something quite different, something about teaching and safety.

The dojo—"dojo" means "place of training" in Japanese—is located in a little shopping center off the beaten track. When you enter, you are greeted by a large quiet space. The room we work in is large and light and airy. Mirrors run almost the length of one wall, windows occupy another, pale mauve carpeting covers the floor. The teacher will be doing a stretch on the floor, or talking in a soft voice to a student. The students will be sitting on a low platform near the door, taking off their shoes and jewelry. We don't have uniforms yet; we're too young.

Class begins on time. The teacher asks us to make a circle. In the beginning we learn names, but after the first few meetings we go right into the warm-up. The exercises are classic—neck, shoulders, elbows, wrists—then the lower body, stretches for the hamstrings, inner thighs, back. We do leg swings, sit in the frog position, shake everything out from time to time. It is regular. First this, then that. Stretch, shake loose. The left, the right. Relax.

Our bodies in the circle occupy less than a quarter of the room. Air and space circulate around us. We move together, straining now and then into the stretch, but at our ease, relaxed. The instructor's voice, soft, unemphatic, simply expects us to follow the commands, which we do without fuss. Warm-up's over.

Line up four feet from the wall. Time for review. First the traditional framing postures: the "natural stance" called *shizen tai*; the "ready position" called *kyotsuke*; and the bow, *rei*. Each school has its own bow; ours, I think, must be one of the best. These formal positions, repeated before a sequence of karate movements is executed, have a calming, comforting effect. The commands heard again and again establish a pattern—*shizen tai, kyotsuke, rei*. Each time you know something has been learned: I know this posture; I know this word; when asked I can perform these motions. *Shizen tai, kyotsuke, rei*. See? Again and again.

All of karate is like this. The martial stances and movements as well as the ritual preparations possess a formal quality, an unvarying regularity and precision, that make them resemble ballet. But the essence of the forms is not in the spectacle they create but in how they feel to the practitioner. *Shizen tai, kyotsuke, rei* are a mode of experience that creates a context for experiences to follow. They carve out in air, in time, in nerves and muscles and flesh, a mental territory, a chamber in consciousness where it is safe to be.

At each lesson we practice what we've learned the time before. Many repetitions, but not so many that we get tired out. Not so many that we get bored. Is your foot at the correct angle? Does your wrist lie flat? Are the hips square? There's enough to occupy attention here. And each day we learn something new: a stance, a turn. The new position is broken down into its parts: where the head is, where the shoulders are, how the weight is distributed. Fine points are elaborated on, briefly. Now and then, there's a little joke. We practice. Slowly at first. If it is a motion, the motion is segmented into steps—one, two—but in Japanese—*ichi, ni*—until we are sure. Then when we have the feel, a little faster, the whole thing done on one impulse. And we move across the floor: *ichi, ni*, and so on, and back again. One more time.

I find the orderliness and safety of these procedures blissful. The world is a dance as we move across the floor. There is no way to go wrong. When someone makes a mistake, it is called a good thing. That's how you learn. We do an exercise in which we deliberately do the step wrong in as many ways as possible. You find your stance by making it too wide, too narrow, too short, too long. Mistakes are good. The way to learn.

People are corrected. Back leg straight, Carla. Foot more at an angle, Jane. The corrections don't matter; they are completely impersonal, part of the dance. We are praised together. Excellent. You're doing extremely well.

We make a final circle. Review some terms: *kiba dachi*, horse stance; *zenkutsu dachi*, forward stance. Then maybe a short announcement. Any questions? Class is over till next time.

———

For the past four years I have been doing experimental teaching. Abandoning the well-travelled roads of lecture and discussion, trying this, trying that. Each experiment a throw of the dice, breath held, heart in throat. Every semester I am pushed (from within) to do something more radical, more daring than the semester before. How's it going to turn out? Every time, I'm afraid it won't work. It's exhilarating, this seat-of-the-pants pedagogy. The rewards are deep; the price has also been high. Karate now poses an example of a pedagogy that is entirely different, if not in aim then certainly in affect. A classroom free of fear. Pedagogy as the creation of a safe place. The karate class embodies the diametrical opposite of the decentered, nonauthoritarian classroom I have ventured to create, where I step back, the students take control, and no one knows from one class to the next what is going to occur.

In karate, all authority is vested in the teacher. But not really in her, for the true authority lies behind and beyond her, in the discipline itself. In karate you are all servants of the same master: the tradition, the discipline, the rules. As my teacher put it one day, there is only the path, and people at different points along it.

In one sense, studying karate is like learning a Western science: definite, sequential, unvarying, first this step, then that. A set of building blocks, facts, rules, principles to be mastered, each one in turn, before you can go on to the next. With this difference: karate is practiced with, and in, the body. The steps alter the person who performs them; you become the tradition, you become the rules. You become your own master. Perhaps there is a parallel assimilation of mind to materials in chemistry or physics so that one's life patterns shift and shape themselves to, say, the electron dance, but if so, I don't know about it.

My point is that karate—formal, external, abstract, calculated— seems at the opposite pole from everything intimate and personal; yet because it requires your total concentration, body, mind, and spirit, and because it requires endless practice, day after day, it enters into the fibers and molecules and knits itself up with your life, trellis and vine. Though it begins and is carried on in the physical realm, it ends by training your soul.

For me, karate's fascination lies in its opposition to the pedagogy I have been practicing whose aim is to allow the student's true self to emerge by removing the structures that enforce imitation and dependency. In karate, it's the reverse: to liberate the self by imposing a rigid set of formal constraints. The aim and the means to it are coherent in both cases. The difference is where you begin, or what you begin with.

My premise, discovered in the classroom, is that the students I teach have already been schooled too much. They work hard, try hard, listen hard, obey hard. It's as if they'd all been taught karate at an early age, before they could decide for themselves whether they wanted to learn it or not, and were now going through the motions, while their minds and hearts, in some cases unbeknownst to them, were elsewhere. For such students my class serves as a wake-up call. Good morning, students, do you know what your desires are? The justification for what I do depends on my analysis of what they need: to start listening to themselves, rather than to someone in authority.

To be empowering, discipline must be chosen. At some fundamental level, if you have not chosen it, the skills a discipline may give you are not yours, are not an outgrowth of who you are, but a disposable proficiency, a bit that could be dropped from your script without being missed. What my teaching has been aiming for is not the empowering discipline itself but the wisdom to know what that might be when it comes along. You might say that it is pre-karate. Which is saying a lot, since to know which course of training is the right one and to be able to choose it for yourself require a great deal of courage and self-knowledge; these skills are indispensable to the mastery of an art. Perhaps I should add that "knowing" may include allowing the discipline to choose you.

There are aspects of karate I would like to incorporate into my teaching. Mainly, the safety factor. By which I don't mean the safety that you feel because of having learned the art of self-defense, but the safety that the teaching of karate confers upon students while they are in class.

This is not a simple matter.

When I was experimenting wildly in my undergraduate class, I went to a conference in Seattle that was full of people interested in teaching. As I went around telling people how frightened I was by what I was doing, implicitly and explicitly asking for help, person after person would offer me their techniques, their advice, which I pretended to accept gratefully. In fact, I was 1) jealous because they all knew more about this kind of teaching than I did, 2) afraid I was floundering disgracefully under the guise of bold experiment, and 3) resentful that they should presume to offer prescriptions for my oh-so-special class. To save my pride, I concluded that to have had these techniques and this wisdom in advance would have prevented the very thing that had made the class valuable: the fear of not knowing where we were going, what we were doing, or what would happen next, which forced us to bond with one another, the way people do in boot camp or in other stressful circumstances. *Because* we had no techniques we became a unit, special to ourselves, never to be reproduced.

I was right, as far as that went. Reading for Yourself was special, and I will always love those students. But karate has taken me round a corner and shown me a new vista where pedagogy is concerned. I thought to myself: perhaps it is possible to create an atmosphere of freedom and safety together. Perhaps the students don't have to feel so frustrated at the beginning of the semester, and I won't have to eat my heart's fear for lunch every day. Perhaps there is a way to develop trust and companionship without the vertigo; perhaps there is even something concrete I can teach them, even if it is only the classroom equivalent (yet to be discovered) of *shizen tai, kyotsuke, rei.*

———

Yet when autumn came, things turned out differently. Inspired by the revelation, conferred on me by my students—that poetry is magic, that it awakens the soul, and that its true expression in the life of the reader is some form of creativity—I embarked on a course designed to put these insights into practice. My voyage was still in progress; I needed to go further from shore. It wasn't yet time to come about and head for any port. And besides, as Ishmael says in the book we were about to read that semester, "I love to sail forbidden seas and land on barbarous coasts."

161

14

LET'S GET LOST

It was the best course I ever taught. I even got the course description right. So the students who signed up—twelve graduate students, three undergraduates—had self-selected for it. Things began slowly, as always, but even on the first day, when they were in small groups, there was an excited hum in the room.

When I reach back in my mind for what happened next, there's nothing. I kept no journal of the course because I was happy. For me course journals are a way to keep fear under control and to rationalize impending failure. When things are going well, I don't keep one.

But records or no, it's hard to tell a straight story, hard to get at the reality of what happened in a class, either on a given day or over time. Anxiety and desire for success distort the record. Wanting to succeed, I gloss over difficulties, forget things. At the same time, being prone to a victim mentality, I frequently rush in to admit failure. Embracing defeat, mentally, before anyone else can criticize me, I end up obscuring the truth in the other direction. When I embarked on my experiments in teaching, I thought I was putting the performance mentality behind me by putting students at the center of things. But now I see that the experiment itself became my performance. Only now my success or failure depended on the performance of the students. The ego's need to be reflected *one way or the other* intrudes everywhere.

The other problem in telling the story is, I can't do it in anything like an objective, reportorial manner. Or rather, I could, but it wouldn't mean anything. I've realized that the story of this course is about issues that have long lain dormant in my life, at the bottom of a pool inside me, like monsters in a fairy tale. They control the agenda here. And the story will come out or not according to their desires. The good news is, that having discovered these backstage artistes, having had to acknowledge the dimensions and depths of classroom experience, I know that not only this course but all our teaching, what we do in class day after day, is a text—beautiful, strange, many layered, frightening—woven out of the memory and desire of every person in the room. We never look at this tapestry, almost. It hangs there on our collective mental wall, oscillating gently, sinister, inviting. Its brilliant, darkly textured world is worth the risk of entering, despite the danger. Let's get lost.

What I have are images—of the students' faces, of their voices, of memorable moments; they come in spurts—peaks and valleys of emotional intensity. Even now tears well up inside me as I write. I loved the course so, and the students, well, they felt all different ways about it. I wanted them to love it as much as I did.

At the end of Sylvia Ashton-Warner's *Teacher* there's a chapter that begins with this anecdote:

What is it, Little One?

I kneel to his level and tip his chin. Tears break from the big brown eyes and set off down his face.

That's why somebodies they broked my castle for notheen. Somebodies.

I sit on my low chair in the raftered prefab, take him on my knee and tuck the black Maori head beneath my chin.

"There . . . there . . . look at my pretty boy. . . ."

But that's only a memory now. A year old.

The anecdote is cryptic at first. The words of the child, awkward and painful. By the end of the chapter, when she quotes them again, we know what they mean. Ashton-Warner's ideas for teaching children, the methods she's built up with so much love and work and imagination over the years, have been rejected by the authorities. Her little school has been torn down. In its place a grand one, where children who used to dance and cry and laugh and sing and paint and argue and shout, now sit quietly in rows.

At the end of my course last fall I felt like that: "They broked my castle." They, the students, the ones I'd been so proud of, so happy for, after all we'd done—the singing, playing, shouting, painting; on the last two days they tore the course apart. Four mornings in a row I cried over what happened so I could get through the rest of the day. Now the whole thing sits in the back of my throat, waiting to be resolved.

So let me begin again.

First, Ocracoke.

The name of the course was American Literature Unbound, and the idea was that we would use the texts we read, *Moby-Dick* and *Beloved* (only those, for the course was to be uncluttered, unrushed, a pure opportunity for absorption in great works of literature—time to wallow in and be drenched by their beauty and profundity, nothing in the way); the books were to be used as avenues *into* the world, rather than as a retreat from it. The books would lead us into all kinds of experience, especially sensory, imaginative, and emotional experience—the kinds that usually get left out in school. So Ocracoke (one of the barrier islands on the North Carolina coast) was to introduce us to the sea, or rather, since everyone had seen the ocean before, it would be a way of realizing, physically, something important about Melville's novel. A chance for Ishmaelian reverie, a combination of water and adventure.

The other purpose of the trip was to provide a bonding experience. I'd learned the previous fall that there's nothing like an overnight trip to make students and teacher feel more at home. It puts relationships on a different basis. You can't be intimidated in the same way by people you've slept in the same room and shared a bathroom with; the experience changes your relationship at a molecular level.

The deep text was my own need to feel accepted by the students. To be part of something they were part of. Not to be alone.

We meet on campus at 4:30 A.M. in front of the chapel. I get there a little late. Almost everyone's there. Three female students who have banded together act as combination mothers and teenage gigglers—they've brought coffee in thermoses. Someone's brought donuts. Someone's brought bagels and cream cheese. Thank God! They're coming through. Everyone shows up. Four cars. Four designated drivers—me, Mark, Ryan, and Bernard. Excited, uncertain, half-asleep, we nervously check directions and bundle into the cars. We're late. All in a row, we barrel off into the morning darkness. We have exactly four hours to make the ferry.

Charlie, a young man from the law school, and James, another law student, both smart, alive, with-it kind of guys, are in the backseat. In front, Sonya, an exchange student from Germany. At first it's awkward, but Sonya and I discover we can talk, so we do. Charlie and Jim converse sporadically in back. After worry about following road signs has worn off, the road unfolds steadily before me. We're doing it. We're on the way. Fifteen people going to an island on their own recognizance. No one said we could. No one said it was OK. We're just doing it because I thought it would be fun to try, and the students were willing.

They planned the whole trip. Ferry reservations, cars, drivers, estimated costs—food, gas, lodging—estimated travel time, itinerary, directions. Feng Liu, from the People's Republic of China, has booked the motel at a remarkably low rate. Paula, from Iowa, has organized most of the rest. New York Sarah has stepped in at crucial junctures to take responsibility. I'm in good hands.

We make it to Kinston, our halfway stop, on schedule. I turn into Bojangles. They don't want to sit—just pee, get biscuits, and go. Off again. Now it's light, the driving's easier, and Charlie takes the wheel. I sit in front with him. It's fun. But time is short. Around Beaufort we lose sight of the other cars. We're late. We're barreling down beautiful roads now—the bay waters sparkle, marshlands spread right and left, tiny towns whiz by. If they're still behind us, we'll never make it. On the long bridges and empty straightaways there's no sign of them. But Charlie drives like a demon, and when we get there—there they are! They took a shortcut. Paula's negotiating with the ferry people. She's got us on. We're the last cars on the ferry. It's heaven.

On the ferry, water stretching everywhere, high sun, seagulls, wind. We explore the boat, cluster in little groups, nap. I doze in the back of the Oldsmobile, Zarena sleeps in front. The trip is long—two, two and a half hours—yet it doesn't seem that way.

I've never been to Ocracoke before but I've heard about it for years. A barrier island, I read in the book I've brought, is something solid that's always changing. The way to preserve it is to let it be destroyed. "In my end is my beginning."

The harbor is bright, the buildings sharply etched and clean. On the lawn of the Visitors Information Center stands the vertebra of a whale, humongous—Moby-Dick! We've come to the right place. Inside we read about pirates. A kind elderly man gives us directions to the beach and to the motel. We're on our way.

Blackbeard's is attractively funky and down-at-heels. Roomy and warm and friendly. All the men in one big room on the first floor. The women split between two. I'm in a room with the students. Off to lunch.

The beach at Ocracoke is clean and empty, a long straight stretch of grayish white sand backed by a long dune topped with pale green grass.

166

The ocean is gleaming blue gray green, and playful, not rough. Early on I worry about students drowning—there are no lifeguards—but they all seem OK in the waves. We swim and sun, drink sodas, take walks. I've asked them to spend some time alone. My alone time takes place on the dune top, hunkered down near some bushes in a hollow of sand. This place seems miraculous to me. Round shiny leaves of bushes, thin spears of faded grass, the smooth surface of untouched sand. The precision and exactitude of outline, the contrast of textures, the delicate palette— life here seems intense, perfect, and abundant. A miniparadise.

Back on the beach I start to worry. We're doing nothing. I ask myself, "Is this education?" But what can you do on a beach so beautiful but enjoy it? Isn't that the point?

At night we get down to work. No. At night we carry out something that looks like a classroom activity. First we make a fire on the beach. (I'm proud of this. I brought the wood from home; Paula called the park ranger and found out whether fires are allowed.) I've brought my guitar. We pass around a bottle of rum someone's bought (what sailors drank in the nineteenth century). I sing the whaling song I know and try to teach it to them. Pass the guitar around. Sing some more. Then the assignment: to relate a significant experience we've had with water. This is the best part—I think—although the stories alone are not what works the magic. The almost full moon rides at the center of a huge night sky, the breezes are soft, the fire glows, I savor the cigarettes I've been bumming from Sonya, and the rum is warm. The sharing of stories—some read aloud from a written text, some told from memory—is somewhat formal, more or less embarrassed, always revealing. It draws a line around each person, sets each individual off, even as the night sky and moon, breeze, fire, sand pull us together. And just as the night divides us body from body, the stories knit us up, soul to soul.

The experiences are intense and different one from another. Bernard out with a friend in a rowboat in waves they can't handle, laughing uncontrollably. Charlie running away from home. Sarah Wilburn carrying water from Lourdes. Michael having a mystical vision of the moon over the Aegean while his parents eat and drink in a restaurant. Jim lying all day on the beach in Los Angeles after his sister's suicide. New York Sarah on the dock at night, sensing the presence of a huge fish. Erin ocean-drunk from sailing.

Three things stand out after that. Reading aloud from *Moby-Dick* while we eat brunch in an airy upstairs room with a view of the marsh. Feng Liu reads the same passage as Michael (does he know it?), the conclusion to "The Whiteness of the Whale"—the German accent and the Chinese rendering the philosophical vocabulary with equal strain and equal force of conviction. On the tongues of the students, among the clatter of knives and forks, Melville's language sounds different from itself. Their reading brings out tones and feelings I've never heard before. Breakfast is abundant and delicious. It's noisy in the restaurant, but the language spills over everything, a rich, complex sauce.

Near where the cars line up for the ferry, Ryan discovers a volleyball net on a field of grass between the dock and the ocean. He's brought a volleyball, and the students split into teams. I sit leaning against a stump and watch them. The day is bright and blue. In the background, ocean water. The students stumble and cavort on either side of the net in a mood between mellowness and hilarity. For me, this is the moment of greatest joy. A gift from nowhere. Sheer, unexpected. After a timeless time, the motors of the cars in the line start up; we pile back into ours. The trip is over.

On the way home, I commit an error. We get to Kinston—our halfway stop—and the lead car (Ryan's) pulls into McDonald's. Maybe it's because I'm tired, but suddenly I fling out of my car and over to the hamburger lovers and burst out with a diatribe on the evils of meat eating, cattle raising, and rain forest destruction. I don't normally impose my vegetarian beliefs on others, but in this situation, out of its hiding place comes the desire to rule, comes the need to be right about something. The students are cowed. As soon as I've done it I know I've blundered, but it's too late. On the way to *my* choice (Taco Bell, of all things), we lose one of the cars. Serves me right.

The fit of pique coming out of nowhere should have warned me, I guess. It signalled that there was a bridge troll somewhere in the vicinity, but I looked in the wrong place. I said to myself: "I'm glad that *I'm* the only one who goofed." But it wasn't true. There were some things that the students did that I didn't like. There were the three who stayed late on the beach after everyone had gone back to the motel. Drinking, maybe smoking dope. And two of them had snuggled in the back of the car on the way home. One of them was married. None of my business I said to myself, but I was pissed.

———

What the trip was for the students I can only guess. What it was for me, I know, at least in part. Seeing Feng Liu's head against the sky and dune, chin raised, squinting at the sun through his glasses. Hearing Michael's trained Germanic baritone on the American strand. Rum and cigarettes. Swimming before breakfast. The delicious mixture of omelettes and literary language. Tumbling in and out of cars, restaurants, the group feeling. Beach beauty.

On our return the students' energy was high: they carried the classes on their shoulders like athletes. They were unstoppable. Usually, in my experimental classes, things are still up for grabs and I am still terrified even in the sixth week. But this class was different. I had no fears. It seemed a miracle.

A week or so after we got back, there was vigorous debate over grades. I'd originally offered the course Credit–No Credit—with this kind of experiential agenda, how could I give grades?—but the graduate school had ruled against it. I turned the problem over to the students. One aim of the course, I said, would be to reflect on the mode of teaching the course represented. Issues of power, authority, fear of performing, learning for yourself versus learning for the teacher came tumbling out. Finally a three-person committee proposed that the class get a group grade: that way, they reasoned, the pressure of competition, of individual against individual, would be lifted. It was a joint venture we were engaged in, and the class should stand or fall as a group. Credit would be given for every kind of contribution—for cutting up vegetables for dinner at Erin's, calling motels, pricing rental vans, managing the class calendar—the nuts-and-bolts stuff that courses depend on but that have no cachet academically. In the final week, they would decide together what grade they deserved. I agreed to all this. Besides, by this time people were tired of the subject of evaluation; they had ideas they wanted to carry out.

I'm a little fuzzy on what we did next. Some of it I missed. I'll tell you why in a minute. We had small-group discussion on Melville's rhetoric; there was a videotape on issues of political power and authority composed of clips from contemporary films (Grand Canyon, Malcolm X); there were a series of skits on gender, papers on epistemology and desire. If you'd asked me at the time, I'd have said that the Ocracoke trip had had no clear influence on our understanding of Moby-Dick; the impact was all on the group dynamics. But looking back now, I think the trip affected our relation to Melville. Because all our attention at Ocracoke had been on physical things—getting from here to there, sleeping, swimming, eating—and on psychological-social things—who was getting close to whom, what people were like, whether the class would work—and because when we got back the discussions of Moby-Dick were planned by a different group of students every time, there was no official line to follow in interpreting the novel. It was mine; it was theirs; it was anybody's. The vague iconoclasm of the atmosphere, the sense that no one was checking up on us, being nontraditional and emphasizing sensory experience and physical activity—all this gave Moby-Dick to us permissively. It was come as you are.

To me the class gave permission to enjoy what I'd always loved most about the novel—its language. Until that time, I hadn't realized to what extent I'd hidden my love of Melville's language because I was afraid I'd be ridiculed for it. It hasn't been the fashion to care about style for a long time, and it's never been fashionable to say passionately that you *loved* a novel's language and to go overboard about it in class. But this time round I began the course by reading an entire chapter aloud to the students, the one called "The Pacific" where Melville describes his "mysterious divine Pacific" and how he beheld it for the first time rolling before him "a thousand leagues of blue." It was this language that made me an Americanist.

As a graduate student in the mid-sixties I'd been grading for Richard Sewall's tragedy course at Yale, and one day when he read aloud from the stage in Woolsey Hall passages from the chapter where Melville explains what the white whale was to Ahab, I decided to write my dissertation on Melville's style. "All truth with malice in it, all that stirs up the lees of things, all that cracks the sinews and cakes the brain, all evil, to crazy Ahab, was visibly personified and made practically assailable in Moby-Dick," I'm quoting from memory now. The sentence that did it, that put me over the top was "He piled upon the white whale's hump the sum of all the general rage and hate felt by his whole race from Adam down and then, as if his chest had been a mortar, he burst his hot heart's shell upon it."

I didn't identify in the least with Ahab, not consciously anyway, but it was Ahab's hate so eloquently expressed that determined what I would spend the next year—and most of the rest of my life—doing. I didn't know it then, but what you wrote your dissertation on determined your professional field. I wonder, now, after all these years, why it was the passages on rage that drew me. The description of Ahab's immitigable hate, so abundantly *thorough* and satisfying, could it have called to an anger buried in me, so deep I had no idea it was there? I know the prose of *Moby-Dick* backward and forward now. It's in my bones. I can quote patches and snatches of it, and one long lyrical sentence from a chapter called "The Dying Whale." But I'm still not too well acquainted with the sources of my rage.

Of my long, intimate relation to Melville my students knew nothing. I spoke once to the class, formally, about *Moby-Dick*. A fifteen-minute talk on the characteristic forms of sentences and chapters in the novel, and how these are related to the mentalities represented by Ahab and Ishmael. I rather liked what I said but don't think it made a great impression. But I didn't care. If the students weren't particularly interested in talking about the language, neither was I. I just wanted to glory in it, to revel again, as in the old days, in the genius with which Melville put sentences together. His perfect ear, his sense of rhythm, his feel for imaginative texture, his knowledge of when to keep something in the air and when to close. A friend from graduate school, A. N. Kaul, once quoted to me a line from R. P. Blackmur that has always seemed to me to sum up the truth about Melville's style: "Melville habitually used words greatly." It was so. And this time around, it was enough for me. I didn't need to prove to anybody that I could discourse about epistemology or make dutiful observations about structure and point of view, or justify the chapters on cetology. This time I would just let myself savor and marvel at the unbelievable feats of verbal artistry the novel contains.

Some of this, I think, rubbed off on the class. People started writing poetry and creative prose. Language was in the air; people read things aloud as if they cared how the words sounded. We were *doing* language; not just talking about it.

So what do you think? Should I have told the students more? held forth? given them more to hold onto? I seem to remember a remark or two from the students about being overwhelmed. But I didn't want my Melville to stand in the way of theirs. I conceived my job as allowing them to get lost, and maybe to find themselves, in *Moby-Dick*'s unnavigable maze.

———

What happened next was, my father died.

My father, who'd been in chemotherapy all summer with apparent success, was suddenly given four to six weeks to live, and then next to no time. One week, two weeks. Anytime.

My father loved literature for most of his life. He read aloud to me when I was little, and later on he recited poetry from memory as we did the dishes together. When I was in grade school, he made up stories to tell me and my friends, and after he retired from the telephone company, he wrote mysteries that got published in *Ellery Queen* and *Alfred Hitchcock* magazines.

Though my mother was a reader and read aloud to me too, my love of literature I've always attributed to him. It was his emotional relation to it that stuck. He loved the sounds of words, and the romance of them, and he passed this on to me as surely as he did the shape of his brow. I can hear his voice reciting, with great conviction and emphasis on the beat, "Gunga Din" and "Danny Deaver"—long poems by Rudyard Kipling that nobody reads anymore. I can hear him reading the opening line of Dickens's *A Christmas Carol*—"Marley was dead"—with an intonation that promised such pleasure to come.

As he lay in the medical unit of the retirement community, I read to him from collections of poetry he had around the apartment, Victorian and Edwardian poems, mainly, some Renaissance. I discovered, as I did this, that nearly every poem worth its salt, if it's not entirely about death, has something about death in it. And I discovered another thing, too. There are some books you can read while sitting at a deathbed, and some you cannot. It wasn't a test I would have wished to make, but there it was. Sitting at my father's bedside while he rested or slept, I read to myself from *A Week on the Concord and Merrimac Rivers*, the book we were doing next in my undergraduate class. As Thoreau paddles up the Concord, nattering on about whippoorwills and such, he is never not conscious of some other river and shore to which this one refers. It was in that realm, as I sat and sang with my father, and read to him, and we talked that I felt we were, though our bodies were here in a hospital-like room with faintly pinkish walls and a Greek-looking design that ran around the walls just under the ceiling. Though I had with me a copy of *Moby-Dick*, I was never once tempted to open it. My much beloved and labored over Melville, struggling magnificently to stem the tides of this world, was too tumultuous and effortful to read in the presence of extremity.

———

It's not exaggerating to say that the intensity of feeling I experienced with my American Literature Unbound students was surpassed only by the joy and pain of being at my father's bedside. I had to tear myself away from my teaching to go to him and my mother in Philadelphia, and, once I had, it took three days to realize I couldn't return home for a while. The strength of my reluctance to leave the students took me by surprise. It was as if I were abandoning my own children, choosing between them and my parents. Whether this depth of involvement in my courses is a good thing or a bad, I don't know. All I know is that it was so.

———

I'm not going to tell about the second half of the course. Its structure was the same as the first. Dominated by a fantastic trip, student-conceived and organized, to Somerset Place Plantation near Edenton, North Carolina, where we spent time doing work that slaves had done and wrote about it afterward. (I won't forget the gritty-salty taste of the corn bread we fried in fatback or how Erin looked, her blonde hair wrapped in a cotton turban.) Later in the motel we had a discussion about our own experiences of oppression that was as good a discussion as I've ever participated in. One student found it so uncomfortably intense, she had to leave the room twice; another burst out at the end:

"It's a privilege to be in the same room with you guys!" and then he dove out the door. Talking it over later, the first student, the one who'd had to leave, said: "There were sixteen rooms in that room"—meaning there were sixteen different experiences of that discussion. At the time, though, the only one I wanted to acknowledge was mine.

And that, as Melville would have said, was the key to it all—my refusal to admit that there were sixteen different stories going on simultaneously. I was happy, so that was the only story I wanted to hear. Can you blame me? The course fulfilled old longings that were bound up with my love of Melville, and of *Moby-Dick*. The novel is a protest against cosmic injustice, a defiance of all constituted authority; it played into my ancient sense of victimization at the hands of power. *Beloved* did too, for that matter. So I loved our rebellion against grades and rules and conventional procedures, and I loved the group ethos. For both novels are also celebrations of communion and spoke to my longing to be rid of loneliness.

The student presentations on *Beloved* were antic, inventive. I saw no signs of disaffection, though they must have been there. We watched Alvin Ailey dance videos, listened to recordings of call-and-response songs like those the slaves had sung; some of us joined in. Michael sang "Every Time I Feel the Spirit" a capella, sitting on the floor with his back against the wall, and it was as if his voice was coming straight out of his chest. We read aloud passages from a flail made of paper strips that was passed around the room, each strip with a quote from the novel or a related text. We drew pictures of the box in Georgia where Paul D. had been incarcerated, no two pictures the same. And squeezed ourselves under the table and talked about what it was like to feel trapped, closed in. (Do you see what I mean? Do you see how great it was?) On another day, the students pulled down all the shades, pushed the table over to one side of the room, turned off the lights, lit candles, and we sat on the floor in a circle, reading aloud quotes from *Beloved* that had been passed out to us in advance.

I would like to stop writing right here. For now my throat clenches, and I have trouble focussing my attention. On the last two days of the course, the students read aloud their evaluations. I had no idea. I'd expected celebration, mutual congratulation, fond reminiscence. What they did was criticize. Lack of structure, said New York Sarah; unfocussed discussions, said Hilary; too much time spent planning and arranging things, said Bernard; too much time spent talking about evaluation, said two or three others; not enough disagreement, said someone else; it was utopian to think we could become a real community, said Sonya. There was tension between the norms of the institution and what we'd been trying to do, deliberated Erin. A few students said only positive things, but I hardly heard them. I was devastated. For me the course had been a wondrous series of events; I began to wonder if I'd been living in a dreamworld. When it came my turn—last—with tears in my eyes and a quavery voice, I read my evaluation, full of pride and joy in the accomplishments of the class, and of my own happiness at what we'd been able to do together. And called for a vote. There was no time to talk about what happened. It was time for the grade. The students from the class after ours had been standing in the hall for ten minutes. The class split between an E (in our system, the equivalent of an A), and an E-. For an awful moment I thought I'd have to break the tie, but then Zarena switched her vote to an E, and it was over.

Another person might have taken it better, not been so sensitive. But the students had unknowingly found me out. Criticism was what I'd been trying to avoid all along, criticism of any kind—literary criticism, criticism of myself as a teacher, my having to criticize them. Why else go to the beach, work as slaves, light candles, and put on little plays if not to escape the steel trap of judgment? With creativity and imagination, I thought we could sidestep the need to measure and find fault, either with ourselves or with the texts we read. I wanted to be safe, "safe from the wolf's black jaw and the dull ass's hoof," as Ben Jonson said. I'd been criticized too early in my life and for too long. Now I wanted to be free from judgments and from judging, and I was offering that freedom to the students. But they were still learning how to criticize, and I had been trying to take that opportunity from them.

They got me, all right, maybe in the deepest place. Taking criticism too much to heart, wanting to be free from it entirely. All along I'd known in the abstract that I taught from places inside me that needed healing. Well, here was my chance, in the aftermath of their evaluations, to forgive myself for fearing judgment so much, to forgive myself for wanting to escape. For wanting to be in school and out of school at the same time.

———

Later someone asked me if this way of teaching gave students deeper insights into the texts, or even stronger feelings about them, than the usual way of teaching would. The question assumes that "we," the readers, will somehow be better off if we have "insight" into "them," the texts. For my class this relation was topsy-turvy. The texts became the scaffolding for the building we were constructing. They were the road we walked on to wherever we were going, the road that allowed us to see those houses, that sky, these trees. They were the occasion for the show we put on for each other in our father's barn. Our carnival.

The texts fell to pieces under the onslaught of the students' energy. They gave, graciously, like old pieces of fabric, in several different places. We tore them apart, like animals, consumed their energy and fire to make ourselves live. Sported their great lines like trophies—"How loose the silk. How fine and loose and free"—this one, from *Beloved*, was worn by both Jim and me. By the end of the course *Moby-Dick* and *Beloved* were in tatters, strewn about our collective mental room like something children leave behind after they've played with it.

———

177

Was it a success? What would that be? everybody feeling good at the end? why not? That was what I wanted. But in this case, that would have meant not to have been broken open, like the clam the seagull drops on the rocks from a great height so he can eat it. Not to have felt the pain of failure and so not to have dived into the pool where rage, self-absorption, loneliness, the need for ego gratification, and fear of criticism lurked, waiting.

I said to myself, after it was over, If only we had had those last two days in the middle of the course. If only I'd had the sense to stop around the seventh week and say, How're we doing? How's it going for you? Is there anything you'd like to change? But you see, I'd learned the year before to take the trip in the third week so that the students could bond early. And they had, we had, and our energy was released. In the seventh week people were dying to *do* things, not to criticize and reflect. The course was riding high then, and then I went Philadelphia. . . .

Each course has its own trajectory, its own momentum. You can talk about scheduling the moment of breakdown and self-criticism so it lands where it's supposed to, but things aren't like that. Next time, if I get that one right, some other part of the vessel will burst at the seams and we'll be awash.

How does it end? It doesn't, really. The course ended. We'll never be in the same room together again. But Jim came to my office shortly after that awful last day and took back everything he'd said. Feng Liu came to talk about his Ph.D. prelims, and Maurice about his dissertation plans. Sonya—the one who said we'd failed at community—came to my office and told me not to be dismayed; it was good that the students felt free to criticize the course, a healthy thing. Erin called me up and asked if I'd like to go for coffee at the Columbia Street Bakery. Ryan suggested lunch—we went to Hazel's Home Cooking—we're planning to have lunch again. Sarah W. asked me if I knew a good dentist and if I'd like to have coffee someday; we had a two-hour conversation at Ninth Street. Bernard gave me a chapter from his novel, and I gave him feedback on it at his request. Michael mentioned dinner with some other students when he passed me in the hall, and later he came in to thank me for the course. Today I met Paula, and she said she'd been thinking about me and maybe we could organize a get-together.

One day, after Christmas break, I got this card in the mail. Salvador Dali's *Metamorphosis of Narcissus* on one side, and on the other it read:

The more time I have to think about American Lit Unbound the more I like it. I have been considering how to communicate my gratitude for last semester's experience; however my prose pales in comparison to the attachment I felt toward our class. I came to Duke hoping to find teachers like you and classes like ours. I was challenged, stretched, stumped, excited—but more importantly, I was responsible. I was responsible for our course. It was this onus of responsibility that added an entirely fresh dimension to the course and required all of us to engage in some self-examination. This is not always a pleasant experience, and looking into that pool of water can be startling. Thank you for taking the risk to teach that class. Thank you for extending yourself far beyond the role of traditional teacher. And thank you for teaching me about literature, academia, and myself.

Sincerely,
Mark Grazman

That was Mark's story, a month later.

I, of course, am still wondering what happened. I still want to know why the students couldn't see how great they'd been. What kept them from appreciating all the fun they'd had, their spontaneity, and wit, and gumption? Why couldn't they see that *this* was the earthly paradise? The course was what all the theory and criticism of literature was pointing toward, had hoped someday could be achieved. Why couldn't they understand that we're just like the barrier island, the ribbon of sand, that's always being created and destroyed, always changing, never the same? That we were perfect, and that our imperfections were all that we would ever have?

I'll never know the answer to these questions. But I feel it's OK not to know. To just go on and let the experience be. I cling to the metaphor of the barrier island, which tells us not to cling. When you teach like this, you don't know what failure is anyway, or success. What looks like victory could turn out to be defeat, as well as the other way around. You just do it, as the Nike ads say, and hope for the best.

15

THE WAY

WE LIVE NOW

Teaching as I did, so that the class became a temporary community, woke me up to the kind of community I was living in. I sensed a thinness in the air round me. The contrast between my intense involvement with my courses and the absence of any such relation to my department and university grew so marked that I started thinking about it actively. Why did I have a strong feeling of belonging in my classes, which came and went with each semester, but a comparatively mild sense of attachment to the unit and the organization in which I worked?

This perception coalesced for me one particular day.

I had just come back from a walk down the corridors outside my university office. The halls were carpeted. The lighting was good. Secretaries in the main office occupied an attractive, welcoming space. Individual offices had been redecorated within the recent past. Outside the windows birds sang in the large green trees. It was a Wednesday afternoon in June, and I was looking for someone to talk to. But, with only one exception, there were no professors in the offices I'd just walked by.

The secretary I usually talked to had left for the day—she leaves early in summer. Another was on leave of absence. A third was busy—I could

181

hear her voice in the hall. So I walked back to my office, deflated. A momentary disappointment, but the roots went deep.

That loneliness had long been a feature of my life was something I'd discovered only recently. I'd realized that for much of my life an underlying fear of loneliness had spurred me to meet standards I imagined were necessary in order to win acceptance and approval, and thus to draw to me the company of other people. I don't know whether my sense that the university was a lonely place stemmed from this ancient habit of feeling or if my perception was more widely shared. But my sense was that at least some people felt as I did.

The university had been generous to me in every possible way: I had excellent financial support, good working conditions, a light course load, freedom to teach what I wanted; I was respected. I liked my colleagues. Nevertheless, I was restless and dissatisfied, hungry for some emotional or spiritual fulfillment that university life didn't seem to afford. I craved the feeling that I was part of an enterprise larger than myself, part of a group that shared some common purpose.

To give myself time to reflect on whether I belonged in the university anymore, I had applied for a grant to the National Humanities Center, a place where professors in the humanities can go to do their research, free from the responsibilities of teaching and service to their institutions. My application was approved and, to my surprise, I found myself looking forward to going to work. When I asked myself why it was that I was filled with happy anticipation as I drove down I-40 to the center, why I didn't feel that way about going to school, the answer came down to this: the center provided an ideal combination of society and solitude. I could be with the other fellows whenever I wanted—all (to my amazement) interesting, sympathetic people and able to be so because they, too, were thriving in the center's unpressured atmosphere—and when I needed to work I could go to my office and shut the door. The character of my work began to reflect the benign influence of the environment. At lunch the thirty-odd fellows would share convivial conversation then return to work refreshed, nourished as much by the contact with one another as by the food; in between times we visited at a common coffee machine, so our contact was built into the day's routine. I asked myself: Why shouldn't there be an atmosphere of camaraderie, opportunities for companionship alternating with solitude in the course of a normal university day? And why shouldn't the spirit of the institution be like that of the center, summed up in the two rules the director gave us at the beginning of the year: whatever you need to do to get your work done, do it; and help each other.

Of course there are obvious reasons why one's home institution can't compete with a special center where workplace happiness is concerned. All the things we fight over in our departments—salaries, teaching schedules, leaves, promotions, administrative jobs, research budgets, course relief—were nonissues at the center. When there's nothing to compete for, peace can reign. Besides, there's no history: no residue of hurts, antagonisms, resentments, and suspicions that people who have been together for any length of time carry around with them—unless the issues that cause such feelings have been dealt with as they arise, which is rare. So, whereas in a normal workplace you have all the potential for the complex feuding that goes on in families, at a place like the center, it's shipboard romance. You can be intimate with people, risk yourself, because nothing can be used against you later, and your livelihood isn't at stake.

Still, the center's atmosphere was nourishing and supportive beyond what the absence of history and things to compete for could have achieved. The leadership and staff members consciously worked to make the place welcoming and comfortable for each other and for those who came to spend the year there. They anticipated people's needs and met them in advance. They made people feel important and cared for. Most of them seemed to like their own jobs. Walking into the building you felt that somebody was minding the store.

It is this deliberate attention to quality of life in the workplace that is missing from most universities I have known, and especially a consciousness of how important it is to establish and maintain good human relations among people who occupy a common space. You might call it an absence of social and emotional housekeeping: looking after the relationships among people on the job.

———

When I returned to my university after my year at the center, I was determined to make it a more supportive environment. My first impulse was to be there more. For understandable reasons, most people in my department (English) do their scholarly writing at home. They want the peace and quiet of a place without constant phone calls, corridor noise, and students knocking on the door. But how can you be a member of a community if you're not there? I might not be able to change other people's habits, but I could change my own, so I moved my computer into my office and went there every day. When I wanted solitude, I put a DO NOT DISTURB sign on my door and turned off the phone.

Next I decided to find out who else cared about the issue of community and form a group. I knocked on doors, made phone calls, walked into offices out of the blue. I talked to secretaries, administrators, professors, and graduate students. I discovered all kinds of interesting, alive, intelligent people I hadn't known before. I thought, There's hope.

Soon I found a partner in the enterprise, a professor from another department. We made lists of who we though might be interested, deciding to keep it small in the beginning, and after talking over various people, we agreed on seven or eight. (Even as I tell it, I feel there was something wrong with this process, but I don't know quite what.) The group met four times: three times in the evening, taking turns going to one another's houses, and once in the morning for breakfast at an on-campus hotel.

None of us, it turned out, had exactly the same idea of what was missing at the university. One person was mainly concerned about women on campus; another had the interests of undergraduate students as a chief responsibility. Both were administrators; they dropped out right away. A third hated his dean and thought that ceremonial occasions honoring distinguished faculty might foster a more communal spirit; a fourth represented the interests of special programs administrators who felt marginalized. My partner and I wanted there to be a place where faculty could get a decent cup of coffee and talk to one another. I never figured out what the chemistry prof wanted; he always talked about how lucky we were, and didn't seem to connect with what other people said. There was no common ground. Since we were all from different disciplines, the absence of a shared agenda was fatal. Our busy schedules made it harder and harder to find times when most of us could meet, so we drifted back to our separate spheres. My friend and I formed a rump group that pursued the coffee initiative into the second semester, but when that ran aground, we drifted apart, too.

But getting back to the day I'm talking about, I walked down the halls of my department and felt lonely.

So what did you expect? a voice inside my head pipes up. Of course nobody was around. It was June, stupid. Professors take off in June if they possibly can, glad to get away from grading papers and exams, and going to committee meetings. They need time off to rest and recuperate and prepare for the coming year. They need time to do their research and to write. That's the way things are.

But if school had been in session, it wouldn't have made a critical difference. During the school year only a fraction of the faculty are in their offices at any one time. Now and then you might catch someone in the mailroom and exchange a few words, but only a few, since everyone's schedule is packed, and no one has time to lose. When a faculty member comes to school, it's not to socialize or exchange ideas; it's to teach, answer mail, make phone calls, see students, attend meetings. And since everyone has a different schedule, there's no guarantee you'll see a given person from one year's end to the next. Without mechanisms to ensure that faculty will interact regularly in a supportive and fruitful way, it's easy for a department to become atomized, and for its members to feel adrift, as if they're navigating their crafts over an alien yet still crowded sea.

The patterns I'm describing vary within the same institution. At mine, rumor has it, biology and botany, political science and public policy fraternize and meet to do business all the time. Patterns vary from one institution to the next; small colleges, for instance, differ from this model in ways good and bad. But I believe the situation I've outlined is common in many moderate to large research universities, both public and private, because their value structure actively discourages a communal atmosphere.

At schools that emphasize research (and this is by now a familiar story), each professor is an entrepreneur whose aim is to enhance his or her reputation within a subfield, so that he or she can move up the ladder—receive more money, more recognition, a lighter teaching load, and various other perks. In this kind of competitive, hierarchical system, people's energy naturally goes into their publications and not toward the institution or each other. A lot of excellent work gets done under this arrangement—excellent teaching, excellent scholarship. The trouble is, except for purposes of hiring and promoting faculty and the occasional curricular review, nobody has to talk to anybody, because none of what college teachers do *depends* on anybody else. We have our specialties, we have the library, and we have our fields of research. The dynamic intellectual exchange one might have imagined would be taking place among distinguished scholars frequently fails to occur because everyone is too busy doing his or her own work. Intellectual life exists between the scholars and their computers, between them and the books they read (or skim, quickly, because they're busy writing their own), and not between people of flesh and blood. Besides, what with students to advise, Ph.D. dissertations to oversee, doctoral exams to give, dossiers to review for tenure and promotion, articles and books to vet for publication, to name a few of the obligations university professors share, there's no time for just hanging out.

The sense of always having too much to do is closely bound up with the lack of companionship, the failure of interchange, and with the higher productivity made possible by the technological improvements that have recently entered our lives. Tenured faculty at research institutions come to exist in an elsewhere of print, phone, fax, and E-mail, their true communities embodied only in books or on disk, or at conferences they fly into and out of several times a year. Globe-trotting relationships with colleagues in one's field make for communities that are exciting, but they emphasize—and possibly even contribute to—the lack of just this feeling in the home institution, whose humdrum realities can't compete with conference glamor.

The system perpetuates itself. One year the graduate students in my department organized a symposium where nine people presented short papers on their teaching. The papers were excellent, and everybody stayed within the allotted time. Discussion had only just begun when the chimes tolled five o'clock; whereupon everyone got up and left. I was amazed. No one stayed around for the best part—talking to each other. The students were imitating us! They were going to their computers, or meeting their other obligations so that they could then go to their computers, because that's what you do in order to make it in our profession.

But it's not just "making it" that motivates them, or us. If it were, the solution would be simple: de-emphasize research. I and my colleagues and our graduate students love to read and write; that's why we went to graduate school in the first place. It's love of our work, as much as a lust for success, that pulls us away from each other and from the institution. So we all have our burrows: a comfortable niche where we stay doing our work. Research is "our work," and we do it alone, unless we're in the sciences. Teaching is our "load," which we also do alone, up there in front of the class, unless we've been converted to collaborative learning. And

187

though there are exceptions to this, too, committee work is the dues we grudgingly pay so that we can continue to read and write for a living. It may be that no force in the world is great enough to pull people out of their more or less habitual, more or less comfortable, isolation.

Well, someone might say, maybe professors are people who do best when left to themselves, who were attracted to the profession because they like solitary work; maybe my discomfort is anomalous. But I believe that most people work most happily when they belong to a community of people who are there to support, encourage, and appreciate them. Universities seem to have forgotten this, if ever they knew it—at least in my experience. For the complaints I'm making now from a position of privilege go back a long way.

In 1970 when I went to teach at Temple, a large urban university, eager to do my best and to contribute whatever I could to the institution, I was filled with frustration and bewilderment at the fact that no one noticed I was there. Of course, I wasn't on the tenure track, which meant I didn't count; all I knew was that I counted to myself. The only person who acknowledged my existence was an old professor of Irish literature who used to crack jokes at me as I went by his office.

It was hard to get to know people at that school. My department's hundred and twenty souls, counting part-timers, were housed in a series of once-attractive brownstones that had fallen on bad days; the rooms were cavernous, ill-lit spaces stuffed with battered desks and chairs. Dispersed among four or five of these buildings, the faculty encountered each other only by chance in the mailroom or at department meetings. We all commuted in from somewhere else. Teaching there was about as personal as riding the subway to work, which I did every morning.

I went around that year looking hollow eyed and mouth grim—I was getting a divorce—rode the subway, graded my papers, went to my therapy sessions, and hung in there. I made some friends in the city and some among the junior faculty, so things could have been worse. But they could have been a lot better. They could have been better if there had been a tradition of attending to the quality of our lives as members of a group, if the leadership of the department had taken time to consider what makes people feel valued and cared for. But there was no attempt. It would have been regarded as unintellectual and a frill, the kind of thing children and people of lesser accomplishments might need, but not something that we mighty intellects had a use for.

Looking back, I ask myself, What would have made life in that department more comfortable and rewarding? What, in the atmosphere of the place, in the way its business was conducted, could have made a difference in how the people who worked there felt?

Home and school, school and home. The answer lies in that relation. As far as I could tell, the workplace at that university was regarded as a kind of war zone. It was assumed that life there was bound to be unpleasant, even grim, and anybody who didn't like it that way was soft and selfish. The school was located in a dangerous part of the city, which contributed to the atmosphere of constant, vague embattlement, but that wasn't the real reason for the mood of the place. The real reason was that no one was minding the store. Gradually I got used to the idea that when I went to work, I was going into hostile territory. After a while, I simply took it for granted. I suspect that many people may be accustomed, as I was, to thinking of the workplace as the opposite of home and what home is good for: love, safety, feeling relaxed and at ease. As a new person in my department, I wanted to be treated like a guest in someone's house, and not to feel as if I were entering a war zone. Let me push the analogy further.

When you invite people to your house, you greet them at the door and take them in. You hang up their coats if it's winter, and if they're staying overnight, you help them carry their luggage to their room. You show them where the bathroom is, and when they've settled in, you offer them a drink and a snack, ask if they're tired from the trip.

If they've not been to your place before, you might offer them a little tour, explain the house rules, if there are any, about keeping windows

189

open or shut, letting the dog in or out, when people usually get up in the morning, how to work the coffeemaker. These practical courtesies let your friends know you have their comfort in mind. They are the ABC of human relations, signs that send a message everyone can read: you matter, your needs are important here.

That was what was missing from my experience at the large urban school: a sense that I mattered. For all I knew, I could have disappeared, and no one would have known the difference. This was how the students felt, too. At that school each student was assigned a number—a long number—which he or she had to be able to produce from time to time. My students used to complain, especially after registration, that they were being treated like numbers; they clearly resented it. At the time, I made no connection between my unhappiness and theirs, but it stemmed from the same lack of consciousness on the institution's part.

I don't want to push the domestic comparison too far, but it highlights the element that's missing from the way universities think about themselves: they lack a feeling for the institution at the human level. This is ironic, because people in the academy tend to regard themselves as operating on a higher plane than businesspeople, who, they imagine, have no time for the finer things, driven as they are by the profit motive. But universities are product oriented; it's just that their products are less easy to define and measure than those of manufacturers. Maybe it's because what universities do is so various and amorphous, relatively speaking, that they've thought less creatively about what businesspeople call "product capability," that which enables production to happen in the first place, especially when it comes to addressing human needs for nurture and support.

At the time when I was trying to see whether I could produce a sense of community at Duke, I got interested in organizational development, the movement within the managerial world that pays close attention to the issues I cared about, sending people to seminars and workshops and training programs with names such as Human Interaction, Creative

Leadership, and Interpersonal Skills. One of the most famous of these programs, called TQM, standing for Total Quality Management, emphasized teamwork, nonhierarchical structures, employee responsibility for decision making, fact-based decisions, listening to the customer—in-house as well as outside—and plentiful recognition and celebration of group success. It sounded great. Just what I'd been missing in my own experience. From what I read, the results, in addition to improved product quality and cost savings, were employees who liked to go to work in the morning. Some universities, I learned, had begun to adopt the strategy but mostly in isolated units—for example, payroll—and not systemwide, not where the professors were.

———

Going through my files one day I found a wistful document: it was a blueprint for what I wanted to do when I came back to the university after my year at the National Humanities Center. It read:

What I am looking for:

> a common enterprise
> belonging
> good feelings in the workplace
> a community of hope
> an integrated life

Why don't these things exist now in the university?

> People are isolated from each other and from themselves
> by their individual interests, professional and personal
> by their departments
> by their crowded time schedules
> by the physical distances between them
> by the psychological distances between them
> by the absence of a culture of conversation

191

by the belief that their welfare depends on the work they do in
isolation from one another

How can these obstacles be overcome?

by a commitment to finding a community of like-minded people
by a willingness to pay the price in personal advancement and
scholarly achievement as these things are now measured
by constructing an alternate reward system

Goal: to create a professional environment that is satisfying to
work in on a day-to-day basis

Means: to meet with a small group of people committed to
finding ways of achieving this goal

It's been said, and I tend to believe it, that every movement in the
history of the human race has begun with a small group of people committed to a common cause. So it hadn't been the small group idea that
was at fault. What was it then? My lack of leadership ability? Very
likely. Not knowing how to go about it in the right way? Probably.
Hooking up with the wrong people? I doubt it. The time not being
ripe? Maybe.

I decided to call the 800 number of the National Training Labs (one
of the outfits that helps people learn how to work with groups). I signed
up for the basic course in their Interpersonal Skills Program. "Our emphasis is on improving human interaction as a means of initiating and
facilitating change within groups and organizations," said the brochure.
It said that developing greater self-awareness and sensitivity to others
was the key to effective working relations. It sounded right to me. Sooner
or later, I thought, I would try again.

———

In retrospect, it strikes me that behind my lament for lost companionship lay a dream of perfect unity—a society of loving friends, caring for one another and being cared for, that never was on land or sea. I don't know why, but only very slowly have I begun to realize how utopian a goal this is, and how long I have cherished it, projecting onto other vocational circumstances—working in a hospital, a homeless shelter, a hospice—the closeness and companionship I miss in university life. Perhaps on the job there never can be a society of loving friends. But it is certain that there never can be, in the workplace or out, a group of people that doesn't have to contend with the push-me/pull-you of all human relations. Peaceable kingdoms aren't born; they're made. And that is why it seems to me that the university, like other places of employment, needs to become aware of itself as a social organism.

This would mean that the leadership would become self-conscious about the nature of human interaction on the campus, finding a way to involve everybody—undergraduates, secretaries, janitorial staff, administrators, professors at all ranks, part-time faculty, graduate students, visiting scholars. It would mean devoting time and effort to building good relationships. Right now the culture of the research university militates against the quality of life because such concerns are regarded as peripheral to a university's main business. They're perceived as unintellectual, more or less on the level of housekeeping: things to be done, if they're done at all, by someone other than professors, who think that they shouldn't have the responsibility and most probably would not have the aptitude for it, much less the time. This certainly was my own attitude until recently.

But if research universities like the one I work at are going to become places where people like to come to work in the morning, where the employees have a stake and feel they belong, then they will have to model something besides an ideal of individual excellence—the Olympic pole-vaulter making it over the bar. By the way they conduct their own internal business they'll need to model our dependence on one another, our need for mutual respect and support, acceptance, and encouragement. If the places that young people go to be educated don't embody the ideals of community, cooperation, and harmony, then what young people will learn will be the behavior these institutions do exemplify: competition, hierarchy, busyness, and isolation.

16

COFFEE

Not long after my failed experiment in community, I took a leave without pay; during my semester off I was invited to teach a graduate course at Emory University. I asked if I could give a minicourse—two or three weeks of intensive work, early in the term. They agreed, and I went.

The course—Teaching and American Literature—was extremely enjoyable. It was easier to be experimental away from home, since I didn't feel under so much pressure to succeed. The students were full of ideas. I lived in a small apartment in a motel right next to the campus and devoted myself to the course. In addition to meeting for class, we met as a group, and in smaller configurations, for coffee, for lunch, for dinner, at a row of restaurants that bordered the university.

One day after returning to Duke I was in the dean's office chatting and brought up the subject of coffee. I told him what a good time I'd had at Emory and said if only we had someplace here at Duke where faculty and students could sit down in an informal atmosphere and talk. The dean was interested. It turned out that his next appointment, the vice provost for student affairs, was looking for social activities students could engage in that didn't involve alcohol. The three of us ended up talking about a cappuccino bar where faculty and students could spend

195

time together. The VP even had an idea of where it could go—in an unused portion of the student center that opened out onto a terrace. We went over on the spot and had a look. The space was perfect. The VP volunteered to fund a preliminary design, and I promised to give a thousand dollars of my own money if the university decided to go ahead.

There were the usual obstacles, doubts, foot-dragging; lots of meetings. The Student Center Committee wasn't sure—after all, the Red Cross held its blood drive in that space once a year, . . . and students were used to studying there. . . . They didn't like to give it up. But the dean came up with the money, the head of dining services got behind it, and the project went ahead. Several vendors were solicited for bids. They came and made presentations to the Cappuccino Committee (a small enthusiastic group that saw the thing through); we picked a local outfit with great coffee and baked goods. More meetings to discuss design ideas, furniture. Then, over the summer, the vice president in charge of internal affairs pulled the rug out from under the whole thing. No outside vendors, he declared. We met, we argued, he stood fast.

Finally the head of dining services got the outfit that had won the contract to rent us their equipment and to train our graduate students to run the establishment. The furniture arrived; the café opened. It was a huge success. The next year, a young professor of political science who wanted something similar in the library approached me, and the whole thing started again. We went to the VP for student affairs and the dean, who again came up with money; we got permission from the head librarian and put another committee together. Now there's a second cappuccino bar thriving on campus. This winter the university, on its own initiative, has opened a third.

These places provide something intangible and priceless. Some faint, faint aura of the history of coffeehouses from the eighteenth century to the 1960s hangs about them, some trace of cosmopolitanism and gemütlichkeit. They make possible a looser, less predictable conversation than is possible in an office or a classroom or a cafeteria. They deofficialize things. I meet at the café to discuss student papers with my teaching intern—a graduate student who's apprenticed to me for a term. She has iced cappuccino; I have a mocha latte. We sit on the terrace at a table with an umbrella where she can smoke. The environment alters the nature of our interchange. Topics can come up that might not in a different setting.

Graduate students who teach in the writing program hold office hours at the café. Faculty and students from the science buildings come over. Small classes meet in the booths. Undergraduates go there to study and end up talking to one another. It's not the society of loving friends or the peaceable kingdom, but it feels good. It's relaxed, the scones are tasty, and the smell of espresso as you enter the library and the student center alters the tone of these places. Sometimes I think that bringing up the subject of coffee in the right time and at the right place is the best thing I ever did in my career as a professor.

17

TIME OUT

I was in the garden preparing the earth to plant some cosmos seeds, on leave again, and exploring the possibility of vocational change. I'd already turned the earth over with my shovel and broken up the biggest clods, sprinkled some dry cow manure and peat moss on top, and was in the process of mixing it all together with my garden fork when I caught myself. I was attacking the earth, chopping into it angrily with my tool, grabbing clods that wouldn't break up and squeezing them impatiently between my fingers. I was working at a frenzied rate. There was no reason for hurry, since I wasn't working against a deadline, but I was hurrying anyway, automatically, mindlessly. It was, I recognized, my habitual way of doing things.

What *is* this? I asked. I came out here to relax, to do something physical before doing my usual work—writing, reading. I had wanted to get in touch with something that smelled and had weight and heft to it. I had wanted to be in the sun, breathing the spring air, getting exercise. And what was I doing? I was attacking things, in a crouched position, hurrying, worrying, and not feeling anything—certainly not the sun or the breeze or how the earth felt. The only sensation I had was pain in my legs when I got up to change position.

198

I'd recently become aware that our work lives as professors (or as professionals in any line of work, for that matter) have become dominated by habits that leave no room for camaraderie or intellectual exchange. Intent on accomplishing our professional goals, we look neither to the right nor to the left and end up eroding the quality of our lives as members of an institution. What I hadn't realized was that the manner in which we conduct our lives is even more important than the things we do with them. Whether we spend most of our time on airplanes and at conferences, or in the offices and classrooms of our home institution, we tend to be busy getting things done: writing the chapter, preparing the class, editing the anthology, drafting the committee report. To produce, to be effective, these are our aims.

The desire to achieve and to see ourselves mirrored in achievement underlies the activities that fill our days. And as long as achievement remains the measure of who we are, our lives will inevitably be patterned in a certain way. It means that hurry, busyness, and too little time will be our portion, for we will never think we have done enough. No wonder I was gardening furiously. Since entering graduate school I had rarely known what it was to do work without pressure. Activities that didn't aid me in reaching my goals I characteristically regarded as interruptions.

When we think about improving the quality of life in colleges and universities, it's important to take this mind-set into consideration. Unless we change the *way* we do things, by which I mean the atmosphere, the rhythm, the texture of our engagements with the world, it won't matter whether our department goes on retreat every spring, or whether we meet in focus groups, redecorate the office, democratize decision making, or celebrate our successes.

The cappuccino bars that have opened on my campus provide a glimpse of how we relate to time. Mostly, it's students who use them, and mostly they're used for work: meetings, studying, faculty-student conferences. This is good. But when I originally imagined what such a place would be like, I had, I think, an unconscious longing for a work life that had some give in it, in which schmoozing with my neighbors had an accepted place. For this to happen, people would have to have time for talking to each other, or feel that they did. For whether or not you have time is more a matter of perception than anything else. The way we live now, we never feel we have time, in the middle of a workday, for just wandering over to a café, sitting down, and spending a couple of hours chatting.

The notion of *making* time belongs to a mind-set that assumes that more important things must be pushed aside or put on hold while we clear a space for this relatively unproductive activity. At best, the recreational aspects of sitting in a cappuccino bar are conceived as a necessary respite from our labors, a time for recharging our batteries so we can go back to getting work done. It's this way of thinking about our time—regarding anything that is not directly involved in productivity as an interruption—that we need to reconsider.

"While visiting the University of Notre Dame, where I had been a teacher for a few years," writes the Dutch Catholic theologian Henri Nouwen,

> I met an older experienced professor who had spent most of his life there.
>
> And while we strolled over the beautiful campus, he said with a certain melancholy in his voice, "You know . . . my whole life I have been complaining that my work was constantly interrupted, until I discovered that my interruptions were my work."

One might take this quote to mean that the professor needed to get over his impatience with the demands of personal life, not spend all his time on work and none on family, friends, recreation, community service. Most of us, of course, know firsthand, or from close acquaintance, marriages that have been the casualties of tenure, lives disfigured by too much eagerness to meet professional demands. I don't think, though, that the old professor's concept of "interruption" refers to the worklife versus homelife dilemma. I think his idea has a different shape. The acceptance of interruption *as* one's work implies a consciousness not wedded to its own purposes. It implies that we need to have an across-the-board relationship to time that is different from the one we normally have. Achievement orientation, which interprets any time taken from the completion of one's present task as an interruption, is not necessarily confined to the workplace. As the attack mode of my gardening reveals, this orientation can invade every corner of one's existence. This is a lesson I've had occasion to learn recently on an almost daily basis.

What happened was I caught a bad cold that just never completely went away. It would seem to, and then, a week or a few days later, the sore throat, fatigue, and low-grade fever feeling would be back. Fortunately, I was on leave from teaching when this occurred; otherwise I don't know what I would've done. As it was, I did practically no work at all—though I've since found out that what I mean by not working some people would regard as doing a reasonable amount. At any rate, I was constantly lying down, taking naps, canceling appointments, not cooking dinner, and paring my day down to doing one, maybe two things. It didn't come easy.

At first, having given up whatever I was supposed to be working on, I'd be lying down resting, and the next thing I knew, I'd flung off the afghan and was halfway downstairs on my way to the garden shed to start repotting my plants. Over and over, I'd catch myself laying plans to clean out the refrigerator, catch up on my correspondence, bake a new kind of bread, get those seeds in before it was too late. I couldn't seem to stop myself from trying to accomplish things, or from at least wanting to accomplish them. Since I wasn't working, I felt I needed to be accomplishing *something.* Having nothing at all to show for myself was making me feel depressed and anxious. I began to feel that I was a person of no worth, that I was *nobody,* because at the end of the day I had nothing to chalk up to my name.

I'm taking time to describe this experience because I think my post-viral syndrome, or chronic fatigue syndrome, or whatever it was, is one of those illnesses, like anorexia, that teaches us about ourselves in a general way; they're what Susan Bordo calls cultural diseases, an index to the spiritual condition of the society in which they appear.

The thing of it was, I wasn't really sick. So what was my excuse? How would I answer when the roll call came? Say that I'd "not been feeling well"? I began to think enviously of cancer patients—at least they had a good excuse for not working. There were times when my feelings of frustration and worthlessness were so great that I gave into despair and cried. This turned out to be the best thing I could have done, for it helped me accept my condition.

I began to reconceive the way to live—at least to the extent that I evolved a very different notion of how to think about a day. The idea was to leave the day as blank as possible. At first, this was to ensure that I wouldn't get worn out by doing too many things. But gradually the idea took on another coloration. Instead of seeing unaccounted for time as empty, I saw it as full, full of peacefulness, absence of pressure. Full of the possibility of lingering, meandering, dreaming, puttering, being lost in thought. The blankness of a morning in prospect began to take on luster. I learned to preserve it from encroachment. The encroachments would come of their own accord.

I learned how to go out and do just one errand. The urge to piggyback—drop off the dry cleaning on the way to the post office, pick up the dog food on the way home from the bank—had to be resisted. One thing at a time became my motto. I began to like the feel of an uncluttered foray into the world, a one-pointed mission. Sensitive to the mental anxiety that accompanied a trip involving multiple stops and several transactions, I decided: sufficient unto the trip is the errand thereof.

With the cessation of outward busyness, inner phenomena became more apparent. I learned to watch myself at traffic lights, to watch my impatience come out, bare its teeth, and pounce. Listening to the pompous canned music American Airlines plays while I waited for someone to answer the phone at the frequent-flyer desk, I watched my impatience grow huge, like the Incredible Hulk. For the first time I saw my feelings of indignation at any kind of delay as vicious rather than righteous because for the first time I didn't assume that my time was being wasted. I was living in a clear calendar, so my impatience, released on its own recognizance, was revealed as the ugly dog it was.

Now let me skip to lunch. One day during this period I had lunch with my meditation teacher. I had invited him, and he had accepted, and we met at a little place called Bread and Board. We sat and talked for two and a half hours; I never wanted to leave. After the first hour and a half I became peripherally aware that the normal time for having lunch was over and that either of us could, within the limits of courtesy, have made motions to leave. But by the rhythms of our conversation, lunch wasn't over, so the exchange continued to unfurl itself freely into the afternoon. The feeling of luxury, of opulence, that that engendered, of having plenty of time, of being in a generous relation to the day—not parcelling out little segments, so many minutes for this, so many for that—made a deep impression on my mind.

A few weeks later I had lunch with a graduate student who has become a friend. We sat on my back porch on a Thursday afternoon. At a certain moment, around the time of the "normal limit," I began to be restless; an old alarm clock inside my head went off, saying "It's time to go back to work." Upstairs there was a paper to write, dissertation chapters to read, the usual pile of correspondence. For a few minutes I wondered how long he would stay. Then the realization the old Notre Dame professor had had came over me: this *was* my work. Not in the sense of being an assignment, but in the sense of being both what I wanted and what I needed to be doing at the moment. I relaxed. The conversation acquired for me a slightly different texture: it mattered less which way things went, who talked, what exactly was said. It had more play in it; in fact, from then on the entire day had more play in it. I had a sense of elasticity in relation to events, a sense that I could handle them deftly and spontaneously the way a good outfielder handles a ball.

The sense of play makes me wonder about my former, my normal, our usual ways of thinking about time. As, for example, that it can be divided into segments into which activities can be fit. Twenty-five minutes for this, two hours for that. This way of conceiving time and its relation to activity is the opposite of the one I felt during the lunches I've mentioned. In what I'll call the lunch conception of time there is no inside and outside, no activity that is fitted into a certain time period as into a box. It isn't so much that you lose consciousness of time—an experience common enough—but that you have a different sense of it. I felt that time and what I was doing were interdependent. I had a sense, in the old sixties phrase, of going with the flow.

The metaphor of going with the flow contradicts the way our culture imagines work and time. In the small office of Autos by Precision, Sales and Detailing, on 15-501 Bypass in Chapel Hill, I recently saw this sign: I MUST DO THE MOST PRODUCTIVE THING POSSIBLE AT EVERY MOMENT. The sign evokes in me the idea of an immense, unrelenting effort to be continuously laboring. Time, on this account, is like a natural resource that it is morally reprehensible not to exploit to the limit. Or, to change the figure of speech, time is like an angel we must wrestle with unendingly.

In statistical terms, workaholism is on the rise. According to Juliet Schor, a Harvard economist who has studied work in the United States, Americans work 20 percent more now than they did in 1970. My friend Lou Lipsitz, a political scientist at the University of North Carolina at Chapel Hill and a practicing psychotherapist, believes that people use work to avoid surprises. They think they can keep everything under control that way, keep the unknown at bay. And he adds: the university is full of middle-aged professors who are depressed. They're afraid to try something new.

The Raleigh News and Observer reported recently as part of a statistical survey it was doing that people in most Western European countries have between thirty-three and forty paid vacation days; Americans, with only twenty, are in a class by themselves. On a visit to Oxford University, I couldn't help noticing how much time, by our standards, the students and professors there spent socializing in pubs and restaurants, or just out and about. Compared to us, they led a leisured existence.

It may be that I have reached a stage of life where I don't have the energy to work that hard anymore. Or lack the incentive, having achieved something that passes for success. Or it may be that I am suffering from some form of burnout. All of the above are probably true. But as a consequence, or, perhaps, quite of its own accord, my sense of reality has begun to change where questions of work and time are concerned. More and more I believe in devoting myself to the moment. Less and less can I support activity that is purely instrumental—do this now so that later you can do that. Less and less do I hold with a conception of education as instrumental—overwhelmingly preparatory, something that enables a person, later on, to do something else. Nor do I believe that educators should lead lives that involve continually evacuating the present moment, hurrying from one activity to the next, borrowing from Peter to pay Paul, always tilted toward the future, always a little off-balance, always a little harried in the here and now.

Stress management is not the answer but a prolongation of the disease. What is needed is a wholly new relation to time and to the way we lead our lives. At some level, this means giving up the desire to control our time and letting go of the need for accomplishment.

Not long after I had entertained these reflections, I was driving down the road on the way home, listening to a country music station on the radio, when I heard a refrain that summed up the situation exactly:

> I'm in a hurry to get things done,
> I rush and rush till life's no fun.
> All I really gotta do is live and die,
> But I'm in a hurry and I don't know why.

Learning to sit still has been difficult—neither reading, nor writing, nor doing household tasks, just sitting. But keeping the attention open rather than occupied gives a new shape to one's experience. Little by little the foreground and the background start to even out. The still presences of rooms, their furniture and decorations, the trees outside one's window, the outdoor scene, these are no longer spaces within which something more important occurs but alternate objects of attention, no less significant than the project you're working on or the conversation inside your head. The nature of one's thoughts starts to become more noticeable as well.

Becoming more aware of my physical and spiritual needs, and more aware of my surroundings, has made me more skeptical about the way we teach our students inside colleges and universities. There's too much emphasis on matters related exclusively to the head and not enough attention given to nurturing the attitudes and faculties that make of knowledge something useful and good. Thinking these things over, I've begun to form some ideas about the kind of place a university should be.

18

THE CLOISTER

AND THE HEART

I've been struggling with the concept of college as a cloister. I know not every university enjoys this privileged seclusion. I went to a college that did—Bryn Mawr—and taught for many years at one that didn't—Temple University. What I have to say applies more to the first kind of school than to the second, but it's relevant to most institutions of higher learning because most of them emulate what the cloister stands for: a place hallowed and set apart. It was the experimental courses I taught at Duke, courses in which I got to know the students much better than I did when I taught in the normal way, that led me to question the usefulness of college as a cloister and also to see the cloister as a missed opportunity. It was those courses that let me see how cut off from life the students were, how cut off from the world they were about to enter, and at the same time, how cut off from themselves. It was also those courses that recalled to me the tremendous passion that the quest for knowledge had aroused in me when I was an undergraduate.

When I was in college, I didn't worry much about what would happen afterward; and as far as I know, neither did my friends. Either you got married, or you got a job, or you went to graduate school, in which case you had a scholarship or your parents paid. The issue seemed straight-

207

forward and not a problem. Besides, what happened after college had very little reality while I was still in school.

The opposite is true for undergraduates today. They seem tasked and shadowed by the future. My student, Shannon, who confessed that she hated to read, but had come to Duke because if she hadn't, she thought she'd end up at McDonald's, is not the exception but the norm. Students who go to schools like Duke are afraid that if they don't get an expensive, high-status liberal arts degree, they'll end up in a low-level job, usually conceived as working for a fast-food chain. And even if they complete the four years successfully, they're afraid of not finding a job when they leave. The other day, crossing the quad, I heard one female undergraduate say to another, in a wail: "I'll be unemployed, have no place to live, and be a hundred thousand dollars in debt!"

Many students, driven by the fear of not getting a good enough job after they graduate, make choices that go against the grain of their personalities. One student I had who was an actor and loved the theater was majoring in economics. When I questioned him about it briefly, he seemed not to have considered a career that would make use of his talents. It was as if his love of the theater and his career plans were on two separate tracks. Over and over I've been surprised to learn that a student in one of my classes was planning to attend law school or medical school—vocations that seemed to bear no relation to his or her aptitudes or interests.

Over time I've come to think about my undergraduate students, whom I treasure and admire and have tremendous affection for, under the metaphor of a train journey. Someone, a parent or other influential adult in their lives, has given them a ticket. On it is stamped medical school, or law school, or business school, or in rarer cases, graduate school. They're on the train and holding this ticket, the countryside is going by very fast, and they're not getting to see much of it. All they know is that when the train arrives at their stop, they'll be getting off.

My experimental courses were about helping students to discover who was holding the ticket so that they could make up their own minds about whether the destination was right for them. More than once, a student would explain why it wasn't right and then turn around and hotly defend the choice anyway. What my experiments revealed was how pressured the students felt to perform in a way that would get them approval from their parents and their peers. They seemed to have little knowledge of themselves, little knowledge of what possibilities the world had to offer, and little sense that they really could choose on their own behalf.

This last point, the students' sense of not being agents on their own behalf, troubles me the most. I think it's the result of an educational process that infantilizes students, takes away their initiative, and teaches them to be sophisticated rule followers. Of course, as professors, we don't see the ways in which what we do as teachers narrows and limits our students: for we ourselves have been narrowed and limited by the same process.

From the teacher's point of view, the classroom is a place of opportunity. Here students can enrich themselves, are inspired, motivated, made curious, enlightened by the professor. Here students participate in producing knowledge themselves, since most professors nowadays would agree that students need to be active learners. The great example of student participation in the learning process is class discussion. From the teacher's perspective, class discussion constitutes freedom. It gives students a chance to express themselves. Instead of the teacher talking, the students talk. They air their opinions, exchange ideas; they disagree with one another, and sometimes they even disagree with the instructor. They raise their hands, they speak, their voices are heard.

But one day my cousin, Jane Dibbell, and I were talking about teaching—she is both a lifelong teacher and an actress, whose view of the classroom is sensitive to its theatricality. She started to mimic what happens when students talk in class, and a new vision of classroom dynamics opened up for me. She raised her hand and began to wave it, her voice filled with anxiety: "Am I smart?" she said. " Am I really smart? Am I the smartest?"

In class discussion, students compete with one another for the teacher's approval. They seek reassurance, and they want to be rewarded with praise. It's a performance they're engaged in, not a spontaneous utterance, and a performance on which a lot depends: their own self-esteem, the regard of their fellow students, the good opinion of the teacher, and ultimately their grade and their grade point average. There are many ways to fail.

You can go wrong by parroting what the teacher has already said, or by *not* repeating what she's said. You can use the wrong vocabulary or misunderstand the question. You can appear so knowledgeable that the teacher becomes uncomfortable and the other students jealous. You can find out to your surprise that nobody agrees with you. You can say something inadvertently funny, and everyone will laugh. You can come across as naive and dorky, a nerd. . . .

Practically everything about you is open to inspection and speculation when you talk in class, since, in speaking, your accent, your vocabulary, the intonations of your voice, your display of feeling or lack of it, the knowledge you can call on, or not, all contain clues about who you are—your social class, ethnic background, sense of yourself as a gendered being, degree of self-knowledge, the way you relate to other people. You can seem aggressive, defensive, shy, manipulative, exhibitionistic.

My cousin was right in intuiting the theatrical nature of the college classroom. People who take the classroom seriously have invested themselves in perfecting a certain kind of performance. Knowing just how to answer the question, performing exactly right for the teacher, learning how not to offend the other students become the guidelines for success in life. Slowly, with practice, the classroom self becomes the only self. At preprofessional colleges where students (largely as a result of parental influence) are headed for law school, medical school, business school, graduate school, the performance mentality intensifies; people are so grade conscious and worried about doing well on their LSATs, MCATs, or GREs, that how they do on tests and papers becomes the measure of their worth as human beings.

My point is that classroom learning can constrict a person's horizons even as it broadens them. Learning too well the lessons of the classroom exacts a price. Its exclusive emphasis on the purely intellectual and informational aspects of learning, on learning as individualistic and competitive, can create a lopsided person: a person who can process information efficiently, summarize accurately, articulate ideas, and make telling points; a person who is hardworking, knows how to please those in authority, and who values high performance on the job above all things.

Everything I have learned in the last ten years has shown me that this is not the sort of person to become. But the educational deck is stacked against becoming anything different. Keith Johnstone, the British playwright, director, and teacher of actors writes of the destructive effects of schooling:

> I tried to resist my schooling, but I accepted the idea that my intelligence was the most important part of me. I tried to be *clever* in everything I did. The damage was greatest in areas where my interests and the school's seemed to coincide: in writing, for example (I wrote and rewrote, and lost all fluency). I forgot that inspiration isn't intellectual, that you don't have to be perfect. In the end I was reluctant to attempt anything for fear of failure, and my first thoughts never seemed good enough. Everything had to be corrected and brought into line.

It's the people who are most susceptible to authority who suffer the most from their schooling, and who must liberate themselves later on from its effects. Many of those who do not wake up to their condition remain in school as teachers, pleased with the rewards of having performed well, so the codes of the classroom are passed on.

The *format* of higher education, its mode of delivery, contains within itself the most powerful teachings students receive during their college years. But most college professors, being products of the system, have given little thought to the ways in which the conventions of classroom teaching stunt and warp students as well as enabling them to expand their horizons. Johnstone writes,

> One day, when I was eighteen, I was reading a book and I began to weep. I was astounded. I'd had no idea that literature could affect me in such a way. If I'd have wept over a poem in class the teacher would have been appalled. I realised that my school had been teaching me *not* to respond.

When I look back at my schooling today, I see what Johnstone sees—a person who was taught not to feel. The long process of coming back into possession of my feelings, learning to recognize their presence, then learning to express them in safe situations, allowing them to be there instead of pushing them down as I had always done—*this* education has dominated the last several years of my life. When I look at my undergraduate students, I see how their schooling is forcing them into the same patterns I have struggled to overcome: a divided state of consciousness, a hypertrophy of the intellect and will, an undernourished heart. I see how compartmentalized the university is, with the philosophy department at one end of the campus, the gymnasium at the other. I see how conditioned the students are—though not terminally so—to keeping their own experience out of the learning process. And I am filled with an inchoate yearning for integration.

But I hear the voices of my friends and colleagues saying, *Aren't you forgetting how much you wanted to become an intellectual? Aren't you forgetting your old love of knowledge? of books and ideas? Aren't you turning your back on something precious? And aren't you forgetting how hard it was to enter the gates of academe, to become an initiate, to learn the trade so that you could take part in the central activities of your profession?*

What about all the people who are eager to have even a glimpse of the life you seem so willfully to throw away?

Isn't your discontent the result of too much privilege?

I listen to these voices and I want to say, Of course, of course; each person's situation is different. Many people did not suffer what I suffered, or enjoy the advantages I enjoyed. My critique of school comes from my experience of it, which is limited, as all experience is. Yet I believe that the lesson I learned holds good for many people other than myself. Human beings, no matter what their background, need to feel that they are safe in order to open themselves to transformation. They need to feel a connection between a given subject matter and who they are in order for knowledge to take root. That security and that connectedness are seldom present in a classroom that recognizes the students' cognitive capacities alone. People often assume that attention to the emotional lives of students, to their spiritual yearnings and their imaginative energies, will somehow inhibit the intellect's free play, drown it in a wash of sentiment, or deflect it into the realms of fantasy and escape, that the critical and analytical faculties will be muffled, reined in, or blunted as a result. I believe the reverse is true. The initiative, creativity, energy, and dedication that are released when students know they can express themselves freely shows, by contrast, how accustomed they are to holding back, playing it safe, avoiding real engagement, or just going through the motions. Besides, it's not a question of repressing or cutting back on intellectual inquiry in school, but rather of acknowledging and cultivating wholeness. As Maria Montessori wrote in *The Absorbent Mind*, education is not just "of the mind," nor should it be thought of as "the mere transmission of knowledge. . . . For what is the use of transmitting knowledge if the individual's total development lags behind?"

The real objection to a more holistic approach to education lies in a fear of emotion, of the imagination, of dreams and intuitions and spiritual experience that funds commonly received conceptions of reality in this culture. And no wonder, for it is school, in part, that controls reality's shape. The fear of these faculties, at base a fear of chaos and loss of control, is abetted by ignorance. For how can we be on friendly terms with those parts of ourselves to which we have never received a formal introduction, and for which we have no maps or guides? The strength of the taboo can be gauged by the academician's inevitable recourse to name-calling when emotion, spirituality, and imagination are brought into the curricular conversation: "touchy-feely," "soft," "unrigorous," "mystical," "therapeutic," and "Mickey Mouse" are the all-time favorites, with "psychobabble" and "bullshit" not far behind. The implication is always that something mindless, dirty, and infantile is being recommended, which in a certain sense is true, since the faculties in question have not been allowed to mature and remain in an unregulated state. The concern that things will fall apart and no one will learn anything if these unruly elements are allowed into the picture stems precisely from their historic exclusion from our system of education. The less we know about these unpredictable domains, the less we want to know.

Throughout this discussion of the compartmentalization of learning, two themes have been running parallel to each other. One concerns the intense focus on performance, geared to the perceived necessity of gaining a foothold in a fiercely competitive marketplace; the other concerns higher education's exclusive emphasis on intellectual development. As things stand now, these two emphases reinforce one another; there are very few ways to excel academically, and thus to become marketable, that include attention to creativity, self-knowledge, and compassion for oneself and others.

I became so interested in this problem, which I called the problem of preprofessionalism, that I came back from leave and created a temporary job in order to study it and report on it to the deans of liberal arts at my university. The process of gathering information was revealing in itself. Like an animal loose in the forest for the first time, I roved at will and discovered how little I had learned, in the course of my academic life, about what goes on in a university. I talked to people who, as a full-time professor, I'd never gotten to know before: the dean and assistant dean of academic advising, the head of the Career Development Center, the head of Counselling and Psychological Services, the vice provost for student affairs, the deans of residential life, the university chaplain, the resident advisors in the dorms. I found that these people did essential, life-sustaining work, that they gave of themselves generously, that they had been thinking for some time about issues that were new to me, and that they were generally under-recognized and underpaid.

Professors, I realized, are the Chinese emperors of the institution—with students as the crown princes. Without knowing it, I had occupied an isolated, privileged space, unaware of what kept the institution running day to day, ignorant of the lives my students led outside the classroom, of the people who helped them when they needed help. I had been generally uninterested in these matters, which, I tacitly assumed, were being taken care of by people with intellects and qualifications vaguely inferior to my own—for if not, wouldn't they have Ph.D.'s and tenure-track positions?

This hierarchical structure, which places people who take care of students' emotional, physical, and spiritual lives lower on the ladder than people who deal only with their minds, kept troubling me as I went about my business. I didn't know what it had to do with the problem of preprofessionalism, but it wouldn't go away. Finally, some months later, it dawned on me that the hierarchy reflected exactly what I felt was wrong with undergraduate education. It depreciates those aspects of being human that are missing from the curriculum and from our pedagogy. The way we perceive the process of schooling—the mastering of skills and the ingesting of information by disembodied minds—is reflected in the way we organize the institution.

This is not lost on the students themselves.

Not surprisingly, the students I talked to in my researches had by far the most trenchant critiques of the university, since they are less invested in it than faculty and staff, whose income and sense of identity largely depend on the institution. I met with various student groups and talked with individual students and soon formed a picture of the problem as they see it. The students complained of the tremendous pressure they were under to get good grades in order to be competitive in the rush to professional school and on the job market. They were headed in this direction so that they could find work, work that would pay back their loans or satisfy their parents, who wanted to see some financial return on their $100,000 investment. So much in the students' experience seemed constrained by this motive: they chose majors that would satisfy the requirements of professional school and took electives that would not spoil their grade point averages.

At the same time, students wanted to explore; they wanted to study marine botany, take a course in twentieth-century religious cults, learn Russian, and write short stories. Their advisors told them: "Take what you love." Meanwhile, their parents pressured them to major in economics. One student summed it up dramatically by saying that he felt caught in a kind of schizophrenia. "Duke wants to produce competitive students, and it wants to encourage self-exploration. Sure, students want to 'take what they love,' but people don't want to be beachcombers."

The most ringing critique I heard came from two students I'd taught two years before. I'd called up the students I'd had in Reading for Yourself, who were about to graduate. I wanted to find out what the Duke experience had been like for them, and to see them one more time before they left, for I loved them. I asked: What did you like best about your education, and what would you change if you could?

One of the students had been premed and had gotten into a prestigious medical school; he was planning to go the following fall. His was a success story, but not to hear him tell it. I took notes on our conversation because I was stunned by the harshness of his views.

He began by citing statistics: the university had a 90 percent rate of acceptance to medical school, a 95 percent rate of acceptance to law school, and was, in his words, "a preprofessional warehouse, an expensive stepping-stone." "I used Duke," he said, "and Duke used me. . . . It's like Monopoly, a money mill. . . . Learning is second. Achievement is first."

The bitterness in his tone struck me. "What would help?" I asked. "Someone like me saying the things I'm saying to you," he replied.

At freshman orientation for premed and pre-law students, he said that he had been told what grades he needed to make. The message freshmen ought to get, he said, was "Learn for learning's sake, not just to get a grade."

The other student whose reactions impressed me, an English major, who in the flush of graduation week said that everything about her Duke experience had been perfect, later wrote a long reflective letter in a darkened tone. She, too, began by citing statistics. "Of the 1,400 people in my class, 600 are going to law school in the fall, and 300 are going to medical school." Of the remainder, she said, some would go to graduate school. "I guess most everybody got what they came for—a ticket to some other place."

She continued: "Why aren't we ever encouraged to believe that a liberal arts education is enough? . . . Does my Duke degree lose its lustre if it's not joined by another? The practices of medicine and law and the academy do not need 1,000 Duke students, but the world does." Like the medical student, she felt keenly that her education had had too little application to the world.

The end product of an educational system that fails to help its students find out who they are and where in the world their talents might best be employed is not difficult to foresee. One day I was telling a friend who is a senior partner at a premier Washington law firm about how career driven my students were. He said he couldn't count the number of younger colleagues who ended up in his office saying that they were miserable but didn't know what to do. They'd gone to the best colleges, had gotten the highest grades, gone to the best law schools, made law review, been hired by a top firm and then—it turned out they hated the work. *Hated* it. But they'd never made any independent decisions, had never stepped off the track; they didn't dare leave for fear of being seen as failures. They felt trapped.

I understand the argument that the university can't do everything. Academic courses, it goes, *are* for the mind. Let the home and the church and the psychotherapist and the athletic program attend to the spirit and the body and the rest. We professors have our hands full already trying to get across the riches of our subject matter in fourteen weeks. We can't be therapists and doctors and spiritual directors, too.

What I am asking for is a more holistic approach to learning, a disciplinary training for people who teach in college that takes into account the fact that we are educators of whole human beings, a form of higher education that would take responsibility for the emergence of an integrated person.

I'll never forget an incident told to me by a professor of Portuguese language and literature from UMass Amherst, a dedicated teacher who had been teaching for a long time. One day, she said, she was walking down the street in Amherst when she saw this striking woman crossing the street—the woman seemed powerful and fearless as well as beautiful. Then the professor did a double take. This was the same undergraduate who had huddled in a seat at the back of her language class all semester, never opening her mouth. My friend said she never forgot that moment—how strong and free, full of life and energy the student seemed, compared to the weak, mousy person the professor had imagined her to be, because she wasn't very good at Portuguese.

One way of making education more holistic is to get outside the classroom and off the campus. It interrupts the programming twelve years of classroom conditioning automatically call up; the change in environment changes everything. The class becomes a social unit; students become more fully rounded human beings—not just people who either know the answer or don't know it. Inside the classroom, it's one kind of student that dominates; outside, it's another. Qualities besides critical thinking can come to light: generosity, steadfastness, determination, practical competence, humor, ingenuity, imagination. Tying course content to the world outside offers a real-world site for asking theoretical questions; it answers students' need to feel that their education is good for something other than a grade point average. And it begins to address the problem of the student who has no conception of what is possible after graduation.

The head of Duke's Career Development Center told me: There are two things students trust, their parents and their own experience. If their parents are pressuring them to attend professional school, then the only thing they have to place in the balance against that is some first-hand experience of the world. Staying inside the classroom won't provide them with that. As Montessori wrote in *The Absorbent Mind* in 1915: "The world of education is like an island where people, cut off from the world, are prepared for life by exclusion from it."

All the same, while speaking about the advantages of moving the classroom off-campus, I'm troubled by the memory of my own college days. I loved college, and the main reason I loved it had to do with being in a cloistered atmosphere. Without knowing it, I chose a small liberal arts college for women located in an affluent suburb because it did not ask me to cope with too many new things at once.

It was intellectual achievement above everything at Bryn Mawr, and I identified with that. It was bliss to be in a place where if you scored 100 on your tests, it didn't mean people wouldn't like you. It was bracing to be indoctrinated in Bryn Mawr's ethos: that women not only could but should be intellectuals, could and should compete successfully with men in the world of mind, where, presumably there was no marrying or giving in marriage. So saturated was I in the values emanating from Bryn Mawr's unofficial motto—Only our failures marry (though I didn't take it literally; I knew you could get married and not be a failure as long as you also got your Ph.D.)—that I went to the best graduate school in my field and became a professor.

I realize as I write that one can never second-guess reality, that it's folly to look back and say, I should have done this or not done that. Bryn Mawr's seclusion was probably right for me at the time, all I could have understood and coped with, given who I was. Though who knows? Perhaps if the college had offered a carefully crafted apprenticeship program or the chance to sample a variety of work situations, I might have sprung for the experience and ended up as a social worker or an editor or a journalist. Whatever the case may be, it was a different kind of omission that my education really suffered from, a more intrinsic lack. I wish that the college I bound my identity over to had introduced me to my heart. I wish it had set mercy and compassion before me as idols, instead of Athena's cold brow. I wish I had been encouraged to look inward, been guided on a quest for understanding my own turmoil, self-doubts, fears. How much pain it might have saved me later on.

This was a use for the cloister: to screen out the world and enable the gaze to turn inward in contemplation. For the growth of human beings an environment set apart and protected from the world is essential. But the cloister needs to be used for the purposes for which it was originally intended: quiet reflection, self-observation, meditative awareness. These are the gifts of the cloister that allow the heart to open without fear.

Most institutions of higher learning in our country do not address the inner lives of their students, except as a therapeutic stopgap. To get help with your self you have to go to a clinic and be assigned a psychiatric counsellor to help you with your problem, or, if you are a member of a mainstream religious denomination, you can go to its representative in the campus ministries. As far as the university is concerned, the core of the human being, his or her emotional and spiritual life, is dealt with as a necessary evil, on the sidelines, and the less heard about it the better. We don't want people to think of our students as having problems. But having a problem with your self is the existential dilemma, the human condition. Learning to deal with our own suffering is the beginning of wisdom. I didn't learn this—that is, that I had to start with myself—until I was in my late forties. I could have begun sooner.

The curriculum of American education, kindergarten through graduate school, is externally oriented. Even psychology and religion are externalized bodies of knowledge, with terminologies and methodologies and histories to be mastered like anything else. Every freshman can tell you that Socrates said, "Know thyself," but is she or he then given any way to carry out the charge? Undergraduates, you may say, are preoccupied with nothing but themselves. They are self-absorbed to a fault. Perhaps, but their self-preoccupation is a function of the stage of life they're at; they want to ask the big existential questions, and they want to know themselves in the Socratic sense. But instead of giving them the means, or the incentive, our present system sidelines this hugely important phase of human development and relegates it to the dormitory. Whoever wants to know herself is strictly on her own.

Occasionally in a literature class, or a women's studies class, undergraduates will be asked to write or speak from their own experience. Often they do so passionately, eloquently. But this is a kind of exception practiced in the corners of humanities departments and is widely regarded as "soft," unrigorous, not a substitute for history, methodology, theory, terminology, information. And of course it's not a substitute; it's simply knowledge of a different kind, but of a kind that, although essential to the conduct of every single human life, has practically no standing in our curricula.

I am not advocating a curriculum devoted exclusively to the pursuit of self-knowledge. I too well remember the rapture of my undergraduate days in the east wing of the Bryn Mawr library reading the thirteenth-century Italian poets. I loved the voyage out. It was full of wonder and excitement. But in order to have a balanced, nonobsessive relation to the world outside yourself, some inner balance and self-understanding are needed. Otherwise, your engagement with the world sooner or later becomes captive to the claims of obscure actors to whom you are paying hush money behind your own back. The old unmet demons—anger, fear, self-hatred, envy, you name it—end up running the show, under the guise of doing sociolinguistics, or molecular biology, or tax litigation, or child advocacy, or ikebana, or whatever it happens to be.

Inside and outside, the cloister and the world. We need both. But somehow higher learning has evolved to a point where it offers neither. Neither contact with the world nor contact with ourselves. This has come about because the university has relinquished responsibility for envisioning life as a whole. Instead, it has become an umbrella organization under which a variety of activities go on, but one that has no center and no soul. Correspondingly, the university doesn't see the student as a whole person but only as a kind of cutout part of a person, the intellect—a segment that it services diligently.

I don't know how to bring into being the world I'm trying to imagine here. I can't imagine it, really. All I can imagine are the kinds of adjustments I suggested in my report to the deans, such as: educating parents about the purpose of a liberal arts education, expanding and deepening the role of advisors, introducing more experience-based courses into the curriculum, finding ways to de-emphasize grades. In fact, I'm *afraid* to envision the kind of world my experience has taught me to reach for because I fear it would seem too outlandish, too impossible. I don't think most of us ever try to imagine our ideal world as educators. We're not encouraged to, certainly. I have taught in colleges and universities for thirty years, but no one has ever said to me: "Tompkins, have your vision of an ideal university on my desk by tomorrow morning." When did anybody ever say that?

The university has come to resemble an assembly line, a mode of production that it professes to disdain. Each professor gets to turn one little screw—his specialty—and the student comes to him to get that little screw turned. Then on to the next. The integrating function is left entirely to the student. The advising system, which could be of great help, seems to exist primarily to make sure people don't bollix up their graduation requirements.

Higher education, in order to produce the knowledge and skills students need to enter certain lucrative professions, cuts students off from both their inner selves and the world around them. By not offering them a chance to know themselves and come into contact with the actual social environment, it prepares them to enter professional school but not to develop as whole human beings. Although parents might object—what, all that tuition and no ticket to financial security and social success?—it would be more helpful to students if, as a starting point, universities conceived education less as training for a career than as the introduction to a life.

EPILOGUE:

CHAIR, TABLE, LAMP

When I get up in the morning now, I feed the cat and the dog, make myself a cup of tea, and go into my study to write. I write about my waking moments, the fretful, ever-changeful transition from darkness into light.

The morning writing has an intimacy that is new to me and that I like. Putting down on paper the incomprehensible and confusing time between sleeping and waking soothes something in my psyche and puts me on friendlier terms with myself. To be the almost dispassionate because still sleepy witness of my own most difficult moments, making my pen move continuously across a sheet of white paper, has an effect of reconciliation and cleansing. It also produces a new level of awareness in the process of coming awake, since I know that I am responsible for remembering what happened.

I invented the morning writing exercise in response to an assignment I had given my class—a course called Writing Spiritual Autobiography I am team-teaching with a friend. The aim of the assignment is to help students find a time and place for silence and receptivity in their lives, for listening and restful waiting—not their usual state. We asked them to invent a small daily routine that would provide this space of awareness; the form was up to them. They were to report back, describing the experience of the routine, what it was like each day. No polished prose required. I do assignments along with my students now because it keeps me in touch with the class and because I like to write. This one is a blessing: it's the first time I have integrated my teaching life into my spiritual practice in a formal way.

After two years of not teaching, I am experiencing a certain amount of happiness and peace in the classroom. This is ironic and also, perhaps, inevitable after so much tumult and trauma. Having pretty much made up my mind to retire—the difference between the bent of my life and the ethos of the university having become, I thought, too great to tolerate—I decided to return to Duke for one last year. I had a sense of unfinished business, something in me that didn't want to just fade away.

I chose to teach a course in advanced composition in the fall semester, having sensed correctly that I would be comfortable teaching writing, since I'd written a great deal and felt I had something tangible to offer. Also I wanted to continue my experiments, though in a lower key, to see if I could come up with a format that would let students discover their own desires while at the same time acquiring confidence and skill in the practice of a craft. And, in fact, it did turn out that way.

The relative calm I felt and the relative success I had came, I surmise, from a combination of circumstances only some of which are known to me. The chief one, and also the least definable, is that I had turned a corner in myself and was no longer so afraid of being a teacher. The responsibility no longer daunted me so much. And from the various workshops I'd attended in pursuit of personal growth, I'd acquired some techniques that helped make the classroom a safer place for students, as well as for myself, and still allowed them to assume responsibility. Though fear is still a major feature of my psychic life, it is not as attached as it used to be to what happens in a class. I feel a greater kinship with students, more on a level with them as human beings than I used to, and I know that if I play it straight and listen to what they have to say, nothing much can go wrong.

You might say that my fear has been replaced in a general way by faith, faith that things will work out and that if I pay attention to the moment, without too much pressure to make it come out a certain way, I'll be all right. Sometimes this means asking the students what they think and being willing to let go of previously made plans in favor of taking up the opportunities circumstance provides. And it means trusting my own instincts.

Another thing I've discovered is that I love to teach with someone else. It augments the process of diffusion, the spreading out not just of authority and power but of focus that makes the classroom a more equitable and more permeable space. It means giving up the pleasure of being *the* one, the one all the students are looking at when their attention is turned toward the teacher, but in return there is the joy of collaboration, the relief of shared responsibility, and the solace of knowing that one is not in this alone.

Besides, in a teaching situation, two heads are more than twice as good as one. Both semesters this year I've taught with another person, and both times wrong turns have been avoided, right turns taken, because the other person saw before I did what was coming round the bend, or apprehended more clearly where we had just been.

The upshot is that although I'm moving ahead with my retirement plans and have started reaching out in new directions—offering workshops on a variety of topics, teaching beginning meditation in downtown Durham—I realize I need the classroom as a base. For I'm still learning what it is to teach, and the students feed me.

———

When I write in the mornings, I sit at a writing table I bought several months ago, having done without a desk for some years and dithered over various possibilities for a long time without settling on anything. I found the table in the basement of a local antiques mall and was attracted to it immediately. It is squarish, made of red-toned wide-grained wood, mellow looking, with rounded legs and a few dark stains on the surface. I was told it was a harvest table. I pictured it in an old-fashioned kitchen, piled with fruit, and felt warm inside. The day I went to pick it up, though, its owner was there, a former professor of education at Duke who had gone into the antiques business—they phased out his department some years ago. We hit it off right away. He tells me it is not a harvest table; it is a teacher's desk, the kind the teachers at Duke used to stand or sit behind in class. The stains are ink stains.

Of course.

Along with the table I bought an antique wooden chair, oak, the kind with spindles in the back and a design carved or stamped into the wide crosspiece at the top. On another day, I went to a lamp store that was going out of business and bought an old student lamp with an oak and brass base and a green glass shade that gives off a kindly light. I feel protected by it. Student lamp, antique chair, and teacher's desk with overtones of harvest table. That should do.

LIST OF WORKS CITED

Ashton-Warner, Sylvia. *Teacher*. New York: Simon & Schuster, 1986.

Dickinson, Emily. *The Complete Poems of Emily Dickinson*, ed. Thomas H. Johnson. Boston: Little, Brown, 1960.

Eliot, T. S. *The Complete Poems and Plays, 1909–1950*. New York: Harcourt, Brace, & Co., 1952.

Freire, Paulo. *Pedagogy of the Oppressed*, trans. Myra Bergman Ramos. New York: Continuum, 1970.

Johnstone, Keith. *Impro: Improvisation and the Theatre*. New York: Routledge, 1985.

Koestler, Arthur. *Darkness at Noon*, trans. Daphne Hardy. New York: Macmillan, 1941.

Melville, Herman. *Moby-Dick, or The Whale*, ed. Charles Feidelson, Jr. New York: Macmillan, 1964.

Millay, Edna St. Vincent. *Collected Poems*, ed. Norma Millay. New York: Harper & Bros., 1956.

Miller, Alice. *For Your Own Good: Hidden Cruelty in Childrearing and the Roots of Violence*, trans. Hildegarde and Hunter Hannum. New York: Farrar Straus Giroux, 1988.

Montessori, Maria. *The Absorbent Mind*. New York: Bantam, 1984.

Nouwen, Henri. *Reaching Out: The Three Movements of the Spiritual Life*. New York: Doubleday, 1975.

O'Reilley, Mary Rose. "Silence and Slow Time: Pedagogies from Inner Space." *Pre/text* 11, nos. 1, 2 (1990): 36.

Palmer, Parker J. *To Know as We Are Known: Education as a Spiritual Journey*. San Francisco, Harper San Francisco, 1993.

Stevens, Wallace. *The Collected Poems of Wallace Stevens*. New York: Knopf, 1995.